the fruit of the spirit

a study guide by
john w. sanderson

First printing by Presbyterian and Reformed Publishing Company
1985

Printed in the United States of America

ISBN 0-87552-431-1

To my children

Diane and David, Judith, Laura and Rob

Contents

Introduction

MERE GOODNESS isn't worth much these days. The subject came up in a university classroom, and the professor asked for the name of a good man. After a short pause the class wiseacre said, "Joe DiMaggio." After the laughter subsided, the teacher remarked that this response was in fact typical of American value-standards. DiMaggio was great because he hit home runs, among other things. Other people are great, he said, because they excel in some way or other. Then he asked, "But who is good, period?" After a very long pause someone said softly, "Albert Schweitzer." There wasn't much discussion of it. Everyone seemed to agree. Moreover, the class seemed to feel that there weren't very many good men in the world.

The more I have thought about that incident, the more uncomfortable I have felt. Why couldn't I have mentioned the name of some evangelical who was famous, *not because he was good at doing something*, but because he was of a noble and good character?

Just about that time I began to preach, in a number of churches, a series of sermons on the "fruit of the Spirit." These studies are an outgrowth of that series of sermons. The more often they are preached, the more the conviction grows that teaching of this sort is needed among evangelicals today. We have many yardsticks for measuring Christian greatness, but the fruit of the Spirit is not high on the list. We seem to prefer other kinds of greatness.

Yet the Scriptures place the highest value on the fruit. "Against such there is no law." "The kingdom of God is not food and drink: but righteousness, and peace, and joy in the Holy Spirit. For he that in these things serves Christ is acceptable to God, and approved of men." "He who lacks these things is blind, and cannot see afar off, and has forgotten that he was cleansed from his former sins." The fruit, then, is proof of our redemption.

During my college days, I heard much about "carnal Christians," people who were saved but wouldn't get rewards. We were urged not to be carnal Christians because we would miss rewards! These studies on the fruit of the Spirit impress me that the permanently carnal Christian is a figment of the imagination, invented to accommodate a certain doctrinal viewpoint. One may (and we all do) have carnal moments, but the Christian must have meaningful character growth, or else he is not a Christian.

These studies are addressed to the people of God, not just to ministers. Yet they will not be easy reading. For the most part I have given my own rendering of the texts of Scripture and have not sacrificed what I consider essential points of discussion in the interest of being popular or entertaining. The days are past when Christians can afford entertainment.

An effort has been made to apply biblical insights to the problems of the present day. An appendix has also been added. It is occasionally referred to in the footnotes, and contains suggestions for further study. Although the list of books could be extended indefinitely, only a few have been included in the bibliography for each facet of the study.

It is a pleasure to record my thanks to many for their assistance in preparing these studies for publication. The original draft was given loving and thoughtful critique by Mrs. Colette Grady of Lookout Mountain, Miss Nelle Vander Ark of the Covenant faculty, Messrs. Gary Lindley and David Hawley of the college student body and alumni respectively, and the Rev. Thomas F. Jones. The Rev. Arthur Kay of Christian Training, Inc., assisted in preparing the bibliography; other bibliographical suggestions came from Covenant's librarian, Mr. Gary Huisman. Miss Nancy Evers prepared the typescript, cheerfully working under the pressure of deadlines.

I owe much to my wife, Pearl, and to my children, David, Judith, and Rob, whose criticisms at various stages of the manuscript's development were of great help.

I wish to thank Zondervan Publishing House for its decision to print a second edition of this volume. A few changes have been made in the original text, and four chapters have been added. The additions should bring a new and added dimension to the main thrust of the studies. My special thanks to Mrs. Pam Polk and Miss Sharon Farrow for their help in preparing the manuscript, and to my wife for many helpful suggestions along the way.

the fruit of the spirit

Chapter 1

The Fruit and the Epistle

THE ITINERANT PREACHERS who were visiting in Galatia were not happy with what they saw. The new churches were not "spiritual" enough. True, they had a love for God and a zeal for their new belief, but something was sadly lacking: they were too free, too radical in their religious practices. They had gone too far from the accepted conventional practices of the Jews, and were in fact in danger of throwing over all that was good and wholesome in what Moses had laid down.

The remedy was simple: look to Moses, to circumcision, and the ceremonial law. Only in this way could the Galatians really please God. So the preachers began their systematic work of rehabilitation. Circumcision was reinstituted as the sign of acceptance with God; the Jewish laws became the touchstone of spirituality.

At once they encountered opposition. But Paul, said the Galatians, taught us differently. Why should we listen to you instead of our spiritual father, Paul?

Why indeed! Because, the preachers explained patiently, Paul is ignoring the Word of God. We must follow Moses if we are to follow God, and if we follow Moses we cannot follow Paul. Besides, Paul is only a second-generation Christian. He didn't know Jesus and in fact spent much of his time persecuting the church. So he isn't a trustworthy guide in things pertaining to God. But Moses' qualifications are unimpeachable. Didn't Jesus say, "If you believed Moses, you would believe me"?

And so it went. The Galatians wanted to please God in their daily living and the visiting preachers were persuasive. The outward ceremonies of religion must be essential to true holiness. What really counted in God's sight was circumcision and the keeping of the law.

All went well for a while. A subtle change came over the Galatians and their meetings. A glow of satisfaction, a sense of accomplishment, pervaded their assemblies. Now they were pleasing God.

Or at least some of them were! A spirit of competition in spiritual matters soon marked their gatherings — those who were making greater progress became aware of the slothfulness and laxity of their less zealous brothers and sisters.

Moreover, the more spiritual began to meet together privately to encourage one another in still greater attempts at holiness, and separately they began to pity those whose efforts were at best lukewarm. As for themselves they developed checklists to gauge their progress, and the more checks they earned the more they desired.

It was somewhat frustrating, however. Somehow the assurance that they were pleasing God was wearing a bit thin. After all, the checks on their lists came from the group, and not from God. Hot disputes about who was spiritual, and what was spiritual; about who should determine who was spiritual, and what was spiritual; about how anyone would know who was spiritual and what was spiritual — zeal had given way to pride, then pride to frustration, then frustration to rancor and bitterness.

What had happened to the Galatians? No one seemed to know, and by now the visiting preachers had gone to other cities so there was no one to give the advice they needed.

One man knew, but he didn't give advice. The Apostle Paul who had founded the church, when he heard of the

Galatians' state, sent off a blistering letter, a rebuke but also a plea to the Galatians to break with their present situation and to return to what he had taught them during the early days of the church when he had brought them to truth out of paganism and sin.

His letter seems to be about three things, but they are not three unrelated things. Almost any outline of Galatians will have three great divisions: the first, autobiographical, running to the end of chapter 2 or perhaps a few verses shy of that; the second, doctrinal or polemic, extending certainly to the end of chapter 4, perhaps a bit farther; the third, practical or ethical. In a letter as intensely emotional as Galatians, neat divisions are not necessarily to be expected. But the overlapping is not due merely to Paul's state of mind; it stems also from the fact that the sick souls at Galatia could only be healed by removing the viruses which were causing the sickness. The viruses were themselves related: they were eating away at the foundations of the former healthy state of the Galatians, viz., Paul's integrity and authority as an apostle, and the message which he claimed to have received from God. If these were destroyed, then there could be no Christian conduct such as that described as "the fruit of the Spirit."

Paul, despite the charge that he was a second-generation Christian, had had a firsthand confrontation with Jesus Christ. True, it was different from the experience of the other apostles because it occurred after Jesus' ascension, but it qualified Paul as an authoritative teacher whose message had a force and a character which can only be described as divine (1 Cor. 7:40; 14:37; Gal. 1:8, 9; 2 Thess. 3:14).

As a teacher of the Church, Paul had already come into conflict with error and its champions. *Their* strategy had been to attack his person (1 Thess. 2) or to suggest that his credentials were spurious; or to claim that his message was novel, injurious, or contrary to Moses. Now if Paul were an evil man or if his qualifications were suspect, his message would lack authority, and the infant churches would be cast adrift from the safe haven into which Paul had led them.

Paul's strategy in such conflicts was to base his message on the Old Testament Scriptures, and to stress his claim to be an apostle in no sense inferior to the others.

Hence in Galatians, fully two-thirds of the epistle is given over to the attempt to rescue the new Christians from the error of the Judaizers who had impugned his authority and had sought to enslave the Galatians by a perverted interpretation of the Old Testament. Paul cites the indisputable evidence for his apostleship, and then appeals to Moses' writings to show that he, and not the Judaizers, remained faithful to Moses. He argues: "to accept Moses is to receive my teaching" (cf. also Rom. 10:5-8).

But another, and no less insidious, error faced Paul in Galatia. Departure from his teaching meant departure from the doctrines of grace (5:4). To depart from grace is to depart from following Jesus (1:6). To depart from Jesus Christ results in opening a Pandora's box of every kind of evil and depravity (5:16ff). Hence Paul must show that there is cause and effect relation between grace and faith on the one hand and works on the other.

FAITH→LOVE→GOOD WORKS, OR THE FRUIT OF THE SPIRIT (5:6, 14, 22, 23).

WORKS→CURSE→BONDAGE→WORKS OF THE FLESH (4:24; 5:19-21).

The subtle change that was already coming over the Galatians was an example of this process at work.

Seen in this light, the Galatian epistle becomes a unit, a harmonious whole. Doctrine and practice are bound together inseparably, and Paul's long defense of his apostleship is seen to be, not the vindication of a self-centered leader, but a passionate plea for the safety and security of the souls of the Galatians who were opposing themselves that they "might recover themselves out of the snare of the devil, who are taken captive by him at his will."

So, while the fruit of the Spirit and the doctrine of the Christian life are stressed in chapters 5 and 6, references to them are to be found in every part of the letter. For example, in the introduction (1:1-5) Paul mentions not only his apostleship (v. 1) and the doctrine of the atonement which is at the heart of the teaching of grace (v. 4a), but also and inseparably the teaching that a Christian is *delivered* from this present evil world, and this is according to the Father's will (v. 4b).

So also, in the closing verses of chapter 2 (which may be considered part of Paul's statement to Peter in Antioch, or a command to the Galatians growing out of that speech), Paul contrasts his message and manner of life with Peter's inconsistent conduct, and argues that false doctrine leads to condemnation (2:16), to a false view of Christ's work (v. 17), and to a frustration of God's grace within one's life (2:21). On the other hand, true doctrine leads to purity of life because it leads to Jesus Christ who alone can grant the power for living (v. 20).

Chapter 3 is full of references to practical Christian living, even though it is a defense and a setting forth of the doctrine of justification by grace. The Galatians knew that they had been re-born as Christians by the work of the Spirit and not by virtue of some inner power of their own (v. 3). But now, how were they to live as Christians? By depending on the Spirit's power, or by relying on the strength of their character without the Spirit's enabling? The answer should be clear — the Spirit came as a gracious act on God's part; He called them and united them to Jesus Christ, not because of an inner goodness, or because they were excusably ignorant. It was a work of grace, and they became righteous only by an act of faith on their part, and an act of grace on His part. The miracles which accompanied Paul's preaching in Galatia were not due to their goodness but came as an act of unmerited favor (v. 5). Thus:

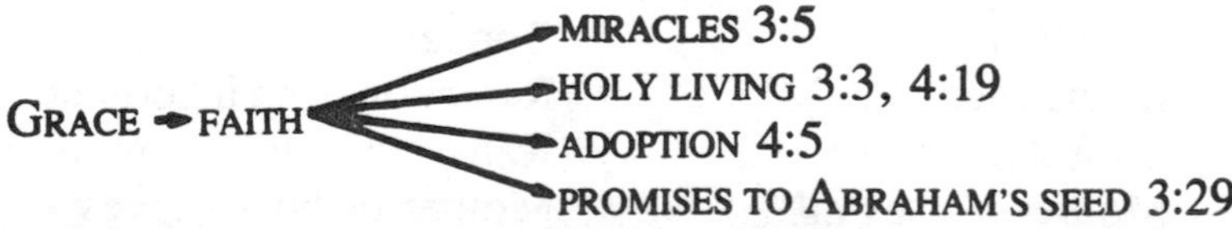

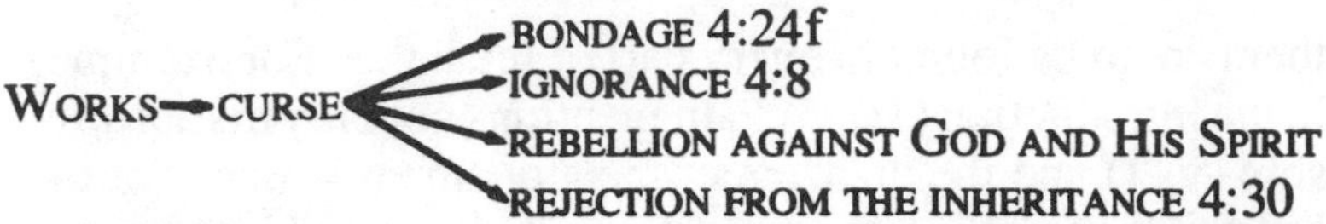

WORKS → CURSE → BONDAGE 4:24f
→ IGNORANCE 4:8
→ REBELLION AGAINST GOD AND HIS SPIRIT
→ REJECTION FROM THE INHERITANCE 4:30

If this epistle teaches anything, it teaches us that conduct stems from a right personal relationship with God, and if the relationship is not right, conduct can only be evil. But how may we properly relate to God? Only by the work of the Holy Spirit. And how and when does the Spirit do His work? Only when Paul's message is preached, believed on, and obeyed.

This explains the emotional tone of the letter. At stake in this controversy is the well-being of the Galatians themselves. Paul had fathered them in the Gospel. Out of a love for them, he speaks passionately to preserve for them and in them the work of grace which had begun with his preaching.

Paul makes all this quite clear in chapter 4:21. He appeals to the law because his opponents *thought* they were appealing to the law. But to show that they were wrong, Paul presents what he calls an allegory based on the story of Sarah and Hagar, Isaac and Ishmael. In v. 25 he uses an expression known to Greek philosophers, Pythagoras and Aristotle, as well as to grammarians. The words "answers to" in some grammatical and philosophical writings are translated "belongs to the same row or column with."[1]

Verse 25 would then read, "Now this Hagar is Mount Sinai in Arabia, and belongs to the same row or column with the Jerusalem that now is" for "she is in bondage with her children." If we follow this clue to Paul's meaning, then we have something like this:

FREEWOMAN	BONDMAID
Isaac	Ishmael
Promise	Flesh
Covenant (with Abraham)	Covenant given at Sinai
Freedom	Bondage
Inheritance	Rejection from inheritance
Jerusalem above	Jerusalem which now is
Mother of "us all"	Mother of bond-slaves
Persecuted	Persecuting

Paul, like the philosophers and grammarians, is putting things which belong together in the same column. Thus, if men follow the covenant which God made with Abraham (which Paul has so clearly expounded in chapter 3) they will find freedom and eternal life; on the other hand, if they keep to the Judaizers' way of thinking and interpret the covenant at Sinai legalistically they are assured of bondage and loss of the inheritance.

Paul's reasoning brings us to several conclusions: first, that the gospel message is one inseparable whole; we cannot have just a part of it. We either have all or none. The Galatians evidently had not fully committed themselves to "Hagar" ("desire to be under the law" is not yet "to be under the law"), but they could not long vacillate between two opinions: either they had to depart from depending on works or they had to relinquish grace and its benefits.

Secondly, Paul's reasoning points up the inseparable relation between faith and practice. Hagar's doctrine "answers to" bondage and rejection from inheritance. Paul's doctrine, however, leads to freedom, inheritance, and the fruit of the Spirit. So we cannot oppose "doctrine." We all have a doctrine! The best thing to do is to make our doctrine clear so that we may examine it in the light of the Scriptures. Since the shadows are falling on western Christianity, we had better know what our doctrine is and why we believe it. Only then will a life appear that is "worth living."

Thirdly, Paul's language indicates that true Christian character is produced by God. It is a growth not unlike the growth of flowers in your garden or of fruit on the trees in your yard. But the fruit can only come from a fruit-seed, and the fruit-seed can only be implanted by God.

Questions for Chapter 1

1. The Judaizers seemed to have a persuasive argument. Do Christians today fall for the same type of reasoning? Give examples.
2. What Old Testament incidents are examples of grace and

of justification by faith? The New Testament itself gives a number of examples.

3. Some people think that Romans and Galatians are "sister" epistles because their messages are so similar (e.g., dependence on the Old Testament, stress on "faith"). Read both epistles and list their similarities.
4. Galatians has been called an emotional letter. Point out the passages where this is most evident. Should Christians today be as concerned about denials of Scripture truth? What issues should arouse us the most?
5. In Galatians the life of the Spirit and the life of the flesh were clearly distinct. Why is there so much ambiguity in Christian living today?

Note

[1] Lightfoot in *St. Paul's Epistle to the Galatians*, p. 181 (Zondervan).

Chapter 2

The Fruit and the Tree

THE VISITORS TO GALATIA had dropped a neat, coherent package of ideas on the churches' doorsteps. Pleasing God is just a matter of doing what He says. If we are faithful to what He says, we shall be holy and He will bless us. We have seen that it didn't work out that way. But how could it fail? If it failed, wasn't the integrity and the power of God's Word called into question?

As we have seen, Paul didn't think so. The error of the Judaizers was that they didn't really know what the Old Testament taught. They thought that Christian character was produced by habitual obedience to rules and ceremonies. Paul said that holiness is something which God plants within men, a seed which develops and blossoms under proper care.[1]

This, Paul contended, is not a new doctrine. It was revealed by God long ago in the very Old Testament the Judaizers thought they were obeying. We turn now briefly to a survey of this Old Testament teaching. Psalm 1 probably comes to mind first: The man who takes time to meditate on

God's law "will be like a tree planted by streams of water. The tree produces fruit at its appointed time, and its leaf does not wither either. Whatever the man does will prosper. But the wicked are not like a tree, but are like chaff which the wind blows away."

Notice how the Psalmist draws a parallel between the godly man and a tree

> If planted by water, the tree produces the fruit expected of it
> and at the proper time.
> If he delights in and meditates on God's Word, then a man
> will prosper in whatever he does.

This is in stark contrast with the case of the "ungodly." Their character is like chaff. (The Psalmist has changed the figure of speech and now alludes to the harvesting of wheat when the wind separates the worthless chaff by blowing it away.) There is no hint here that the tree could ever bring forth anything but fruit; nor that the ungodly could ever be anything but chaff. There is a radical difference between the two — and it is God's Word and man's reaction to it which makes the difference.

Jeremiah undoubtedly quotes from Psalm 1, and he enlarges upon the contrast in chapter 17:5-8:

> This is what the Lord says: Cursed is the man who trusts in man, depending on human nature as the source of his strength. His heart has departed from the Lord. Such a man will be like a heath in the desert — he will not produce good fruit when other plants do — but will inhabit the dried up places of the desert, a salt land where nothing lives. But the man who trusts in the Lord and has no other security is blessed. He is like a tree planted by the waters. It spreads out its roots by the river and is not affected by the heat, but its leaf remains green. Further in time of drought it continues to blossom and never ceases from yielding fruit.

The law is not mentioned here as it was in Psalm 1: instead the contrast is between trust in man and trust in God. But this is not a significant difference: the sort of obedience to the law which the Psalmist had in mind *is* trust in God. "Trust in man" is departing from the Lord. The results of each kind of "trust" may be seen as follows:

> If the Israelite relies on man, he will not see good, will inhabit parched places (like a heath).
>
> If the Israelite trusts in God, he will spread his roots to gain more strength for growth; he has no cause for fear of drought since the brook will not dry up; he will not cease yielding fruit.

Jeremiah has repeated the Psalmist's idea: there is no middle ground, and there is a necessity or inevitability about it all. The man who trusts in God *will* have fruit.

This passage also teaches us that all men believe in and trust something or someone. Jeremiah says, "Cursed is the man who trusts in man. . . . Blessed is the man who trusts in the Lord." There are really only two possibilities, he implies, so that man *inevitably and necessarily* believes. God has made him a believer, and he cannot avoid believing and committing himself to something. The so-called unbeliever believes just as firmly and just as wholeheartedly as the so-called believer. The priests of Baal at Carmel had as much faith in their god as Elijah did in the Lord God. They differed in the object of their faith.

In religious discussions today, faith is belittled. The word seems to be used half-apologetically, and is set over against "knowledge," "science," or "facts," the very mention of which bespeaks confidence, certainty, and conclusiveness.

But the truth is, all men are believers. The scientist commits himself to his "method"; the positivist trusts his "verification"; the TV commercial sells its product by saying, "Science has shown . . . ." They differ from the Christian not in believing, but on what or on whom their trust depends. We stress this because men must see their "idols" for what they are worth. In the day of judgment, who will be the safe refuge, the Lord God or "the final findings of science"?

Isaiah (ch. 5) tells us of a vineyard[2] which, despite every good prospect, produces bad fruit. The owner has spared no effort to make it produce the very best of grapes — he has turned the soil with a hoe; he has removed stones from the soil; he has planted the best vine available; he has built a tower to protect the vineyard from marauders; he has prepared for the time of harvest, by hewing out of the rocky soil a trough for the juice to flow through. And now he waits!

Instead of the full ripe grapes from the cultivated vines, there appear wild grapes, perhaps sour, perhaps small, or spoiled, or unripened. In any case they are utterly unacceptable to the owner. He disclaims any responsibility: "What could have been done more to my vineyard, that I have not done it?" (v. 4). The fault had to be in the vine!

Applying the parable, Isaiah identifies the vine as the twelve tribes of Israel, and especially Judah (v. 7). The fruit which God had expected is "justice" and "righteousness": the wild fruit Judah actually produced is "oppression" and a "cry" for help from the people who were being oppressed (v. 7).[3]

Not content with merely a general characterization of the wild fruit, Isaiah lists seven specific sins which, contrary to all expectation, were the fruit of Judah's life. Each sin is introduced by a "woe" (vv. 8-23). We may abbreviate as follows:

1. covetousness v. 8
2. debauchery v. 10ff
3. arrogance and secularized thinking v. 18f
4. relativism in ethics v. 20
5. pride among governors and rulers v. 21
6. drunkenness v. 22
7. injustice in the judgments handed down by judges v. 23f

But behind all these, there is the disease of which these are but the symptoms: Israel does not regard the Word of the Lord (v. 12) and has rejected the law of the Lord, and has despised His Word (v. 24).

The lessons of this chapter are many. What immediately strikes us is that the sovereign God is not the author of sin. Man's righteousness is a direct result of God's activity; but man's sin can only be explained as rejection of God by arrogant man.

Moreover, although sins may masquerade for a time as

fruit, since they necessarily and inevitably flow from a rejection of God and His Word they soon are seen for what they really are, and God rejects them.

In Psalm 92, there is a contrast between grass which soon perishes, and the palm tree and cedar tree which enjoy a long and fruitful life:

> When the wicked spring up like the grass, and when all the workers of iniquity flourish, they will be destroyed for ever . . . The righteous will flourish like the palm tree and grow like a cedar in Lebanon. They are planted in the house of the Lord; they will flourish in the courts of our God. They will still bring forth fruit in old age; and will be full of sap and green. These things will demonstrate that the Lord is upright . . . (Psalm 92:7, 12-15).

What characterizes the grass is its short life: this is the wicked, the brutish man, the fool (vv. 6, 7). The brutish man is one who lives on the level of the animals, whose decisions are based on what can be seen, and whose desires are always controlled by bestial emotions. The fool is the man who does not like to have God in his knowledge.

On the other hand, the righteous is like a cedar, with perpetual foliage and sweet perfume. He is also like a date-palm in an oasis. Even though he is surrounded by drought and death, he himself enjoys growth and prosperity. The secret of his fruit-bearing is a hidden source of life. His source of life is to be found in the house of God, in the courts of God. The Psalmist has not only frequented the house of God: he carries with him all the time what the house symbolizes: God is really with him, and this is what His house illustrates. So he feels in his heart the forgiveness which flows from the altar; he has been cleansed by the water of the laver; the light of the golden candlestick has fallen on him, and his prayers like incense have been presented to the throne of God; blood has been sprinkled for him on the mercy-seat and in the strength which comes from God's nearness (symbolized by the eating of the show-bread) he will not fear a hot drought from the desert. His supply of grace is perpetual, inexhaustible, and fresh every morning.

The Psalmist does not leave us in doubt as to the reason for this difference between the evil man and the righteous. In v. 1, he calls men to praise God for His lovingkindness and faithfulness. Then in v. 4, he explains why he himself will join them in singing God's praises, "For you, Lord, have made me glad through your work." The "work" of v. 4a is the work of enlightenment, so that the renewed man can see the "works" of vv. 4b and 5.[4] It is God, then, who has made the difference between the man who is "grass" and the man who is the "tree."

We may put it this way: the man who delights in and meditates on God's Word — the man who trusts in God — the man who has been enlightened by God — shall always bear fruit. Here we have the balance found in all of God's revelation. There is no tension or conflict between divine sovereignty and human activity in redemption. "Sanctification is the work of God's free grace, whereby we are renewed, in the whole man after the image of God, and are enabled more and more to die unto sin, and live unto righteousness" (*Shorter Catechism*, #35).

But time is required for fruit-bearing. No Israelite farmer would have looked for fruit before the proper time. Neither then would the Old Testament have concluded that godly conduct could have been produced overnight. Yet, after a while, it was inevitable, necessary, that fruit appear.

Here, then, are major Old Testament references to fruitful living by God's saints. Since Israel enjoyed a horticultural economy, we are not surprised that the Lord used such everyday examples of growing and fruit-bearing to illustrate what sort of character His saints should have.

So John the Baptist was using a familiar metaphor when he preached in the desert, "Bring forth therefore fruits worthy of repentance: and don't say to yourselves, We have Abraham for our father: for I say to you, that God can, out of these stones, raise up children for Abraham. And even now the axe lies at the foot of the trees: every tree therefore that brings not forth fruit is cut down, and cast into the fire" (Matt. 3:8-10).

"Repentance" was John's word for that state of mind

which the Old Testament characterized as "delighting in" and "meditating on" God's law. The Baptist, consistent with his message of judgment, places a heavier emphasis on the absolute necessity of fruits worthy of repentance, connecting it with the day of judgment which will finally distinguish wheat from chaff, reward the wheat and punish the chaff. Again, John stresses the Godward side of fruit-bearing when he tells the complacent Jews that security lies not in being Jews physically (God can make stones into sons of Abraham), but in producing "good fruit."

John as the forerunner of Jesus thus paved the way for Jesus' still more explicit teaching, that fruit is the clue to character because there is, as in nature, a close correspondence between fruit and that which produces it. In the Sermon on the Mount (Matt. 7:15ff) Jesus warns against false prophets and says that we can know them by their fruits. This, He says, is a safe guide[5] because "a good tree cannot bring forth evil fruit, neither can a corrupt tree bring forth good fruit" (Matt. 7:18).

Jesus makes the antithesis even stronger in Matthew 12:33, "Either make the tree good, and its fruit good; or make the tree corrupt, and its fruit corrupt: for the tree is known by its fruit." We should point out here that in both chapters Jesus is using a word translated "corrupt" which should not be interpreted as "rotten" or "decayed." As Arndt and Gingrich comment, "Do 'rotten' trees bear any fruit at all?"[6] They suggest as translations for "corrupt" such words as "unusable, unfit, bad." False prophets will appear, says Jesus, in outward appearance no different from Moses, Samuel, or Isaiah. But because their hearts are false, they can only produce unusable, unfit, or bad fruit (cf. Matt. 15:18-20 and note the similarity to Gal. 5:19ff).

We should bear in mind that these thoughts of Jesus are addressed, not to scholars, but to all of God's people. The evil of the evil fruit will be obvious; and so will the goodness of the good fruit, and God's people will thus be preserved from false teaching (cf. John 10:4, 5, 8, 14, 26, 27; 1 Cor. 14:37).

Jesus is here insisting on that radical change in a man's heart which He called being "born again." It is this teaching which takes Christianity out of the realm of mere ethics and makes it not just a "way of life" but life itself. Fruit is not something which can be superimposed by any external means. It is not to be confused with good habits which a parent forms in his child; it is not something like the conformity to authority which a serviceman soon learns (and seems to resent all the rest of his life!). Fruit is the result of a work performed in man's being by an immediate operation of God, and there is no other way to get fruit. To put it into theological terms — there is an indissoluble connection between regeneration and sanctification, such that there cannot be one without the other. "That which is born of the flesh is flesh, and that which is born of the Spirit is spirit" (John 3:6).

In the gospel of John (12:23ff) Jesus explains what this regeneration is. First, He illustrates it from nature, from the sowing of a seed. The seed must "die" if it is to produce life. Death here is to be understood as a loss of identity, a literal changing of the seed into what it was not before although the matter persists throughout the change.

Now if this does not happen, says Jesus, the seed "abides alone." Westcott says,[7] "In this sense isolation is truly death." The seed which does not germinate is really unusable and unfit. When Jesus applies the figure in the next verse, He says a man who loves his life destroys it! But the radical change which begins with a death really issues in "life" and "much fruit."

In all this the seed is passive. It is sown, and by itself in the ground it is subject to laws set for it by God. Similarly the human soul is regenerated, it is born again. It has as little to do with its new birth as it did with its first.

But there is the man-ward side. In the bearing of "much fruit" man is not idle. God and man each functions in his own sphere to produce the much fruit Jesus predicted. We come to this concept in John 15.

Jesus uses the figure of the vine. It is not a new idea; it was used in Psalm 80:8ff and Ezekiel 19:10ff of Israel as a vine which disappointed the divine Farmer by producing evil fruit. A vine, like a tree, has one purpose, to produce good fruit. A branch finds its true purpose only when it grows on the vine and bears fruit. The farmer's purpose is to cultivate the vine so that it bears a maximum crop. Now Jesus is the "true" vine. In contrast to Israel which did not always produce good fruit (cf. the references above) and therefore was not a "true" vine, Jesus will always produce good fruit: "He that abides in me, and I in him, the same bears much fruit" (v. 5). The Father is the Farmer: He cuts away unfruitful branches (Judas is sometimes called "a son of waste"; cf. John 17:12), and prunes fruitful branches so that their productivity is increased.

This leaves the branches for consideration. Their task is spelled out in the one word, "abide." Here Jesus introduces us to what is called "the mystical union." Paul speaks of it often in Ephesians. Every Christian is united to Christ and by means of that union *and by that union alone*, he enjoys the benefits of redemption. But this is not a passive thing. It involves the activity of "working out" (Phil. 2:13); it is an "exercise" of spiritual powers called into play by God's providence (Heb. 12:11). It is quite specifically an abiding in (or better, a continuing in) the Scriptures which is true discipleship (John 15:7; cf. also John 8:31, 32). Note that Jesus says loving is obeying, and obeying is loving.

This brings the various lines of teaching together. Christian character is not a purely human product, although God uses means in shaping it. It is God's work: Psalm 1 mentions the law, Jeremiah 17 — trust in God, Psalm 92 — divine enlightenment. God unites men to Himself so that there is a continual flow of grace and power which produces fruit, just as sap produces fruit on a tree or vine. Man is to trust in the Word, obey it, meditate on it, delight in it. Under these conditions, fruit is inevitable, and God is pleased with it.

Questions for Chapter 2

1. In Psalm 1:3 what does the word "prosper" mean? By

comparing this verse with its parallel in Jeremiah 17:8, try to grasp the scope of what the Scriptures promise.

2. How long should one wait until some fruit appears? Do you think that some fruit grows more quickly than others? Would fruit grow more quickly in some people than in others? Would one's past life influence the rapidity of the fruit's growth?
3. In view of the fact that there are many fine examples of good character among non-Christians, how may Christians be differentiated from them? In this connection, study Matthew 5:20 and 1 John 4:4.
4. Do you detect any development beyond the Old Testament teaching regarding Christian living when you study such New Testament passages as John the Baptist's sermons or Jesus' remarks?
5. Give some everyday examples of "abiding in Christ." Note that the word translated "continue" in John 8:31 (KJV) is the same as that translated "abide" in John 15:4.

Notes

[1] Cf. the Appendix, esp. Bonar's chapter on "Christ for Us, the Spirit in Us."

[2] The richness and variety of these figures of speech should not take our minds from the lesson which is the same whether the righteous be a tree or a vine, or the unrighteous chaff, a heath, grass, or wild grapes. The *good* fruit is acceptable to God, produced by Him through the agency of His Word, mediated by trust of the individual who is righteous in God's eyes. The *evil* fruit (or chaff, or grass) is not acceptable to God. It is produced by a misplaced trust, through the rejection of His Word.

[3] Delitzsch notes a play on words here: God looked for "justice" *mishpat*, but Judah produced "oppression" *mispach*; for "righteousness" *tzedaqah*, but found instead a "cry" *tzeiqah*. He comments: "The prophet describes, in full-toned figures, how the expected noble grapes had turned into wild grapes, with nothing more than an outward resemblance." *Biblical Commentary on the Prophecies of Isaiah*: Vol. 1, p. 165f.

[4] Different Hebrew words are used in 4a and in 4b and 5.

[5] He uses a very strong word for "know" here.

[6] A *Greek-English Lexicon of the New Testament*, p. 749.

[7] *The Gospel according to John*, p. 180.

Chapter 3

The Fruit and Its Cultivation

"SALVATION" IS A many-sided word. When a man is saved, he is reinstated into privileges which he lost by sin. In the Scriptures, God also promises a man full recovery from his troubles. The many blessings of the Gospel come in different ways and at different times. For example, the rehabilitation of man's character follows a dramatic change in his legal relation to God, and an equally dramatic change in his own nature.

This change *within* man is a many-sided one. All too often we think of it only in terms of the new birth; but there is also the change in man's relations, in his spheres of activities, and in his hopes and aspirations. Since I have already mentioned (p. 28ff) "regeneration," it is well at this point to stress the changes which come from man's new relationships.

In Ephesians 4, Paul speaks of our being related to other Christians in "one body" (4:4). This is not a static relationship but a dynamic one: the body grows, it is being harmoniously joined together (4:16). In this new relationship each Christian has a new function and a great responsibility (4:7). God has given each new Christian a gift, and the entire

Christian community stands in need of that gift! His life takes on new meaning because he lives for the saints and for their welfare (4:12).

Think of what this must have meant to a newly converted sinner like Mary Magdalene. Her life had been empty, meaningless, and guilt-ridden. She had no hope of anything but continued social ostracism. Yet what a change when she met Jesus Christ! We find her ministering to Him and later on to His people. She loved much because she had been forgiven much, and this love drove her to the company of the saints. She now clung to His promises to give new direction and meaning to a hitherto wasted life.

Thus, these two changes provide man with what he needs for a new life: motivation, power, direction, and opportunity for development. We may put it this way:

Motivation —love toward God, and to His image in man.[1]

Power — help from the Spirit, the new birth, vital union with Christ.

Direction — the Scriptures, an enlightened conscience or what the *Westminster Confession* calls "Christian prudence."

Opportunity — God's providence which gives the redeemed man occasions to act and re-act Christianly, that is, according to the teachings of Scripture.

The direction from Scripture is both negative (pointing out the weeds) and positive (calling attention to the fruit). But direction alone is not enough. Man also needs the motivation, the dynamic, and the opportunities for expressing his new character and abilities which were mentioned above. These are also provided in Scripture. The Scriptures, therefore, are preeminently the means of grace. It is important that we see that this is so.

The Word of God is the vehicle by which faith comes to us (Rom. 10:17). This faith unites us to Christ who then justifies and sanctifies us (1 Cor. 1:30) and these acts of His are the source of our power. Faith is a kind of sight; sight produces within us adoration which in turn becomes love (and this is our motivation), which begets the other fruit. Finally, faith as sight enables us to see God's hand in everything, hence by faith we see the opportunities which provide for the exercise and development of our God-given character.

This brief account should emphasize the importance of following the Scriptures for the development of the Christian life. There is no other means for the cultivation of true piety than the Scriptures. Paul, when he was bidding good-by to the Ephesians, entrusted them to God "and to the word of his grace which is able to build you up" (Acts 20:32). Our Lord, in Luke 8:15, said that the seed which fell on good ground was an illustration of the Word's reception by those "in an honest and good heart, having heard the word, hold it fast, and bring forth fruit with steadfastness." And because the Scriptures have a well-rounded character they meet the believer's needs on all occasions: hence there is need for no other instrument in the hands of the Holy Spirit. The *Confession of Faith* (chap. XIV) puts it this way:

> By this faith, a Christian believeth to be true whatsoever is revealed in the Word, for the authority of God Himself speaking therein; and acteth differently upon that which each particular passage thereof containeth; yielding obedience to the commands, trembling at the threatenings, and embracing the promises of God for this life, and that which is to come.

Moreover, all the Scriptures must be read and preached. In theory, most Christians profess to believe that there are sixty-six books within the sacred canon. But in practice, our canons are much smaller. Most preachers shy away from the Old Testament; or if they do preach on such texts, they somehow avoid the Wisdom literature and the prophets. We should read, and preach on, whatever books we believe to be contained in the canon, no more and no less.

Ministers (and their congregations!) should review their sermon subjects every year or so to determine whether they have been serving up a balanced diet. Fathers should see to it that the family altar reading covers all of the Bible. Many people suffer from malnutrition because their diet lacks some important mineral, frequently only a "trace mineral." Is the church of God suffering today because some seemingly unimportant or irrelevant portion of the Scriptures is being overlooked?

Another facet of this problem is the shying away from the warnings of the Scriptures. Some people have little boxes in their homes with cards on which are printed "precious promises." Whether it is good to read verses out of their God-given context is not the question here. What we should desire for ourselves in addition is a set of "precious warnings" which will brace our souls for the temptations of the day.

Robert Murray M'Cheyne once preached on, "Why is God a Stranger in the Land?" He said that one of the reasons was ignorance of the Word of God. Perhaps when we realize how desperately we need the Scriptures — there is no piety, no cultivation of the fruit, no saving of souls apart from the gospel message — then we will become less encultured, more biblical and God will once again become familiar to us.

It will not escape our notice that the fruit of the Spirit is, after all has been said, a description of Jesus Christ. Who truly loves, has real joy, peace, patience and the rest, but the Son of Man?

But He has imparted this nature to us, and the fruit is ours as we look at Him. There is a mysterious chemistry of the Spirit by which we become like what our eyes see. This was illustrated in the Old Testament when men were delivered from death from a serpent's venom when they looked at the brazen serpent Moses had placed on a pole in the camp. John tells us that the complete fulfillment of that type will be when we will see Him face to face — "we will be like him for we shall see him as he is" (1 John 3:2).

But the process is going on now. "We all, with open face beholding as in a glass the glory of the Lord, are changed into the same image from glory to glory, even as by the Spirit of the Lord" (2 Cor. 3:18).

The Christian must see his Lord! and the blessing of reading the Scriptures correctly is to see not mere words however true, but the Son of God Himself. "You search the Scriptures," He once reminded His contemporaries, "because in them you think you have eternal life, and they testify concerning me, and you won't come to me to have life" (John 5:39f).

Jesus is here reminding us of a trap into which it is easy to fall: the error of reading the Scriptures but not finding Jesus Christ there in His glory. In a sense this was what the Judaizers were doing, and the Galatians were in grave danger of doing it. They were studying the Scriptures but missing Jesus Christ. The prayer of every Christian must be directed toward avoiding this trap. Our prayer must be — "Throughout the sacred page I seek Thee, Lord; My spirit pants for thee, O living Word."

In the chapters which follow there will be a section entitled, The Means to Cultivate This Fruit. In each case, some suggestion will be made regarding the strengthening of what God has given us. But also in each case, it will be the Scriptures which will plant, water, prune, and cultivate the fruit. This is why the Reformers so often used the slogan, *Sola Scriptura*.

Questions for Chapter 3

1. Think of many groups devoted to Bible study. Why do they differ from each other so drastically?
2. The Judaizers knew the Old Testament well. Is there something more to Bible study than learning the stories, memorizing some verses and explaining the prophecies? In this connection study John 5:39, 40 in the New American Standard Version.
3. Study Hebrews 4:12, 13. When was the last time you were "pierced" as you read the Scriptures?
4. What motivation do you require so that you will "hunger and thirst after righteousness"?

Note

[1] Cf. the Appendix, esp. Murray's chapter on "The Dynamic of the Biblical Ethic," in *Principles of Conduct.*

Chapter 4

The Fruit and the Weeds

SOMEONE MIGHT have asked Paul, why do you speak so much against works? Don't you want people to be good and to do good? Paul's answer is given in Galatians 5. Briefly it is this, you are putting the cart before the horse. To put emphasis on works first is to insult God by offering Him what is evil. Since He is holy, He can but curse works offered in this way. So (to repeat our diagram):

WORKS → CURSE → BONDAGE → WORKS OF THE FLESH.

The man who is content to offer God his own works produced by his own power, is a man who will be cursed, placed in bondage, and condemned to continue to live apart from the God whose character He has impugned.

Living apart from God, Jeremiah said (cf. p. 23ff.), is to be like worthless desert plants. I have called such plants "weeds" in order to bring out their worthless character. They are worthless because they have no divine life to produce them; they are the products of hatred for God. They may masquerade as fruit for a while but soon their weed-like character will be apparent.[1]

The weeds seem to have begun their appearance in Galatia.

The Christians there had imbibed enough of the Judaizers' doctrine so that weeds were appearing in the garden of the Lord. "If you bite and devour one another, take care lest you be consumed by one another" (v. 15). "Let us not become boastful, challenging one another, envying one another" (v. 26).

Paul wanted the Galatians to see where they were headed if they persisted in the Judaizers' way, so he collected a horrendous catalog of weeds and dumped them onto the front lawn of the Galatians so they could see for themselves. The list is not exhaustive (see Appendix A on page 179).

The evil character of the weeds is obvious, plainly recognized to be evil by anyone's standard. Put it this way: who would ever want a person who did these things for a roommate, a husband or a wife? But this conduct is the inevitable result of rejecting Christ and His grace.

The works of the flesh lead to bondage, the fruit of the Spirit to freedom. Now on the surface it seems the other way around. And many people today looking at Christianity think it a bondage. Of course much depends on what we mean by "freedom." The word as it is often used today means "freedom from . . . ." Somehow today any and every restriction placed on human conduct is called an infringement on liberty. But the newborn infant has an instinctive fear of falling. Somehow he prefers the confinement of his mother's arms to the freedom of dropping through space! Moreover, parents know that the child who has arrived at the "terrible two's" should not be free to roam at will. Freedom in these senses is danger, perhaps death. In addition, freedom from restraint among men leads to chaos, and perhaps mutual destruction. But I do not imply that every structure of support and restraint is good. "Freedom from . . ." has much to commend itself, and indeed this is the great theme of Galatians. Some restrictions, indeed most restrictions, bring us into bondage. The Word of God, understood in the light of Paul's argument in this epistle, gives man support but not bondage, provides him with restraint but not restriction. Paul's emphasis is on freedom to love, to be happy, to do good. Freedom is emphatically not freedom to sin. He develops it this way:

For, if we are free to sin, then each man will live for himself, and in the process will destroy all who come across his path (v. 15).

But, if we are free to sin, then we are not free to enter God's eternal kingdom (v. 21).

As a matter of fact we are not free to sin.

For, a Christian is inhabited by the Spirit and wins the conflict with sin (v. 17).

And, a Christian by receiving Christ has turned his back on sin (v. 24).

Hence, brotherly love is the rule by which a liberated Christian should live; and the power of the Spirit is the dynamic by which he lives.

Now it should be clear that there is no *lasting* value in attacking the weeds hoping to alter them, improve them, or permanently inhibit them; nor can we accommodate them, engage in an armed truce, or a cold war with them. After pointing out that they are self-destructive (v. 15), Paul mentions that they also are destructive of the good seed which God has sown in the world (v. 17). Hence the only approach to the weeds open to Paul is "crucifixion"[2] (v. 24), and crucifixion can come only to those who are in Christ. At this point we have returned to the teachings summarized in the first two chapters of this study. Only God can help a sinful man. Only a supernatural act can deliver man from his evil character and his evil deeds.

This act which Paul calls "crucifixion" has already been mentioned in Galatians 2:20 — "I have been crucified with Christ; and it is no longer I who live, but Christ lives in me; and the life which I now live in the flesh I live by the faith of the Son of God, who loved me, and delivered Himself up for me." This is an oft-quoted verse, but a study of it in context yields helpful insights into the issues before us. Our verse comes at the end of a difficult passage. We may mention two problems: (1) to whom are the words in 2:15-21 addressed? (2) what is the connection between Paul's "dying to the Law" (2:19) and Peter's eating pork?

As to the first, there is much to be said for taking 2:15-21 as the continuation of Paul's speech to Peter "in the presence of all." For Peter is being rebuked for not living consistently with his profession. As a Christian he had died to Old Testament ceremonies, not that they were evil in themselves (after all, God had commanded them) but because their continued use signified that the Messiah had not really come to Israel, and that the Spirit had not come to the Gentiles (Acts 10:45). And particularly when Old Testament ceremonies were understood by some as gaining merit before God (a Judaizing doctrine, not once taught in the Old Testament), such conduct on Peter's part was only "rebuilding what I once destroyed" (2:18).

This brings us to the real situation so far as our confrontation with Christ is concerned. "If, while seeking to be justified in Christ, we ourselves have also been found sinners, is Christ then a minister of sin? May it never be!" (2:17). Christ is not a minister of sin because when we embrace Him and thus abandon the law as a means of justification, we are only following the lead of the law itself! To some the law is a wall which restricts, inhibits, and thwarts all desires and ambitions. In this sense, law only kills.[3] But as Paul uses the word frequently, the law is a door which opens onto the grace of God. He uses it in this sense in 2:19.

See how Paul's reasoning applies to Peter. When he was in Antioch, he ate with the Gentiles, presumably eating pork with them. When some people from Jerusalem came for a visit, Peter began acting like a strict Jew again, i.e., not eating pork with the Gentiles. Why? The chapter does not tell us but we might speculate that Peter's "fear of the Jews" indicated he was afraid of losing favor, or of losing opportunities to speak. Now to be afraid of men is to refuse to recognize that one is dead. Peter had died once, but in Antioch he played the hypocrite and his conduct, in that one particular instance, preached a false gospel, and "frustrated the grace of God" (v. 21) for where the Gospel is perverted, grace is frustrated.

Paul at least is not guilty of any of this. "With Christ I

stand crucified." Hence I will not worry about what people think about, or even seek to please them (1:10 should be read in this connection).

But how does Paul get the strength to withstand temptation? "When I speak of living, I do not mean myself. As a Christian I have been united to Christ." I am a tree planted by the brook, I am a palm-tree in an oasis. I am a branch in the true vine. How did this happen?

"And so far as I now live in the flesh [so Lightfoot] it is a life of faith." Faith is the instrument which unites me to Christ, and in Christ Jesus I have wisdom, righteousness, sanctification, and redemption (see 1 Cor. 1:30), in short, all I need. If I find in Christ all I need, why fear the Judaizers or seek the favor of other men?

All this is what Paul means by "crucifixion"; it is, he says, the only way to deal with the weeds of the flesh. Even this has a twofold aspect. The Godward side is regeneration, such a refashioning of man at the very roots of his being that he is a "new man." He has a new life, new thoughts, new desires and inclinations. He is in every way *new* because God has re-created him.[4] There has been a radical change, a decisive break with the past. The chaff is now a tree; the heath is a cedar; the fruitless vine is now bearing fruit!

But there is also a manward side. The "new man" is not yet perfect. He is a battlefield in which a war is being fought between implacable enemies. "The flesh sets its desire against the Spirit, and the Spirit against the flesh, for these are in opposition to one another, so that you may not do the things that you please" (5:17). Now although we have suggested that the renewed man is a battlefield, it should not be inferred the man is passive, or a helpless onlooker as these two forces fight within him. He is the battlefield, but he also finds himself on both sides of the battle and sometimes he wills to do what at other times he refuses to do. "Irrespective, therefore, of what the believer wants to do, this counterfeiting influence [the resistance of the flesh] is always at work. Hence the new life, too, is subject to a penetrating, internal dualism."[5]

Now his resource in this battle is to "walk in the Spirit" (v. 16); to be "led by the Spirit" (v. 18). This is possible, Paul says, and even necessary because we already "live by the Spirit" (v. 25). What was spoken of in general terms in the Old Testament is here made specific. In the Old Testament, the believer was united to God, and God gave him life.[6]

"In the three expressions ('walk by the Spirit,' 'led by the Spirit,' and 'live by the Spirit') here, the first emphasizes conduct, the second conformity of will to the Spirit's leadings, and the third vital spiritual fellowship, mystical union."[7] The Holy Spirit, by His dwelling within the Christian, provides the motivation, power, and direction the believer needs if he is to produce fruit and resist the antagonism of the flesh.

The Spirit's action is to "root out the weeds" and to water and fertilize the plants. This was done once for all in regeneration, and now it is accomplished progressively in sanctification. The Spirit acts secretly, quietly; He also works in a man's conscious life warning (v. 26), and exhorting (v. 13), for plants and weeds cannot grow together in a Christian's life.[8]

The fruit of the Spirit does not initially take the form of outward deeds, or even of habits of life.[9] Perhaps it will be well to borrow a word from older theologies and speak of "habitudes." More modern synonyms might be "abilities," "sets of mind," "seeds." The fruit of the Spirit is a cluster of seeds which grow and appear at their appointed time. It is only after the sun has shined, the rain has fallen, the weeds have been pulled that the fruit becomes evident and can then be recognized as such. Exercise then produces fruit (Heb. 12:11), and fruit-bearing in the Christian life is just as exact a science as horticulture in a modern vineyard.

Galatians is not the only place where we have lists of the fruit. It should be clear that here is no "official" checklist. It is probably impossible to enumerate all the facets of Christian character. What the apostles do in each case is to list those which are especially applicable to their readers. What led Paul to the enumeration in Galatians was doubtless his pastoral knowledge of the particular needs of the congregation at the time of writing. Note the following:

Rom. 5:3-5	**1 Tim. 6:11**	**2 Tim. 3:10**	**2 Pet. 1:5-7**
steadfastness	righteousness	teaching	faith
approvedness	godliness	conduct	virtue
hope	faithfulness	faith	knowledge
unashamedness	love	long-suffering	self-control
	patience	love	patience
	meekness	patience	godliness
		persecutions	brotherly-kindness
		sufferings	love

(Many of the fruits are repeated in 1 Corinthians 13:4-8, but are expressed in negative terms.)

In 2 Peter 1:5-7, the apostle begins with faith and calls upon his readers to find in their faith a virtue already furnished there; and in that virtue, they will find knowledge; and so on up the scale until love is reached. In our chapter Paul gives "love" a priority as the root and ground (cf. Eph. 3:17) from which the other fruit blossom. We have already anticipated this thought in the diagram on p. 16, the clue for which is found in Galatians 5:6.

We are struck by the fact that Paul does not use similar terms to describe the character produced by the flesh and by the Spirit.

FLESH → WORKS
SPIRIT → FRUIT

"Works" involve labor, and yet yield no benefit. "Fruit-bearing" requires cultivation, but the fruit itself comes from a growth-process which is not directly the result of labor. Yet its effects are valuable indeed.

Paul does not suggest that a specific "fruit" is to replace any one "work." We are dealing with the complexities of the human spirit, and no one knows the heart. The apostle is dealing in each case with outstanding examples of conduct, and no exact correlation should be sought between "fruit" and "work." For this reason in the chapters which follow only such use of the list of the works of the flesh has been made as will assist in our understanding of the fruit.

We will now turn to specific fruit and specific weeds. As we do so, we will try to spell out the conscious processes which Christians must follow in the science of fruit-bearing if the weeds are to be kept down and the fruit is to appear in abundance.

But at this point a warning is in order. Our Adversary sometimes produces in men an artificial fruit, a carnal counterfeit, which confuses people into thinking that they have real fruit, only to discover in the day of judgment that God never knew them (Matt. 7:23). How may we illustrate this? A number of years ago when our children were young, they were exposed to measles. Our family physician suggested that they be given inoculations to protect them. As he was administering the "shots," I asked him how the medication would act, and he replied, "This will give them a light case of measles, so mild that no one will be able to detect it, but enough so they will not contract the real thing." I thanked him for the medication, and also for an illustration.

Satan's tactic is to give some people so light a case of Christianity that they will never get the real thing. Hence it is imperative for us to discern true fruit from artificial fruit, and thus deliver ourselves and others from the judgment, "I never knew you."

The Weed	The Artificial Fruit	The Fruit of the Spirit
hatred	limited love	love
sorrow	temporary joy	joy
anxiety, strife	numbness, carelessness	peace
impatience	laziness, insensitivity	patience
pride	manipulation by kindness	kindness
evil	hypocrisy	goodness
infidelity	half-heartedness	faithfulness
self-seeking	false modesty	meekness
lack of control	choosing lesser goods	self-control

Questions for Chapter 4

1. If Paul were writing in the twentieth century, do you think he would have any reason to add to or subtract from the list of "works of the flesh"?

2. Can you think of a modern parallel to Peter's conduct in Antioch? Should we place any limits on Paul's strategy mentioned in First Corinthians 9:19ff?
3. Why is it that some people are more rigid than others in matters of secondary importance? Is fear the only cause of this?
4. Are all the weeds equally bad, or are some worse than others? What makes one sin "more heinous" than others?

Notes

[1] There may be a superficial difference between "works of the law" and "works of the flesh," as Paul uses these terms. The former may be "decent" and "innocent," good works by man's judgment; but when offered to God they lose their innocent character and are rejected by Him. In time their true character appears and the revolting "works of the flesh" soon make themselves evident. To follow this distinction, I have called "works of the law," *artificial fruit*; and "works of the flesh," *weeds*. Cf. p. 40.

[2] Paul moves back and forth from the literal situation to the figurative description of it. If we keep this in mind, we will not be confused by the thought that "works" might be "crucified."

[3] Note that the ASV correctly translates 2:19: "For through the law I *died* to the Law" (italics ours).

[4] For a detailed study of what we are here covering quickly, the reader is referred to John Murray's valuable study, *Principles of Conduct*, pp. 202-228.

[5] Ridderbos, *The Epistle of Paul to the Churches of Galatia*, p. 204.

[6] We recall the beautiful words of the Nicene Creed: "and [I believe] in the Holy Spirit, the Lord and Giver of Life."

[7] Burton, *A Critical and Exegetical Commentary on the Epistle to the Galatians*, p. 323.

[8] Matthew 13:29, 30 refers to the world; not to the church, not to individuals.

[9] In the training of children we frequently speak of good and bad habits. Unfortunately the word has many meanings, and is susceptible to an unbiblical interpretation. Some of the definitions given in *Webster's Seventh New Collegiate Dictionary* are: "7a: a behavior pattern acquired by frequent repetition or physiologic exposure that shows itself in regularity or increased facility of performance b: an acquired mode of behavior that has become nearly or completely involuntary" (p. 373). Surely the fruit of the Spirit is acquired through an act of God and should never become involuntary!

Chapter 5

Love

"I BEAR YOU WITNESS that, if possible, you would have plucked out your eyes and given them to me. Have I then become your enemy . . . ?" (4:15, 16). "Let us not be boastful, challenging one another, envying one another" (5:26).

What had happened to the Galatians? Under Paul's teaching they had begun well, but the Judaizers' doctrine was beginning to take effect. Their love for one another was dying; the weed of hatred was already in evidence.

But "love" and "hatred" are elusive ideas. Men use them loosely, frequently without any idea of what they mean. To consider all the Scriptural teachings regarding love would fill several volumes. Hence some basis for limitation must be found here. It seems clear that "love" in Galatians 5 refers to that affection which a Christian should have for other men,[1] and so our study will be limited to that aspect. In fact we may profitably confine ourselves to two passages, Matthew 5:21ff and Leviticus 19:9ff, and to such references as are necessary to expound these texts.

The Weed to Be Rooted Out (Matt. 5:21ff)

In enlarging[2] upon the commandments of the Old Testament, Jesus found two perversions in the current understanding of the law. First, what had been commanded was interpreted woodenly, without reference to people as people, so that some laws were applied cruelly, others were applied narrowly so that many sins were considered exempt from them. Second, He found that additions had been made to the law. Some of these were extensions based on questionable inferences (e.g., to love a neighbor came also to imply that one might therefore hate his enemy, cf. Matt. 5:43). Others were added through a desire to protect God's law by putting a fence (i.e., men's laws) around it. Jesus' task in the Sermon on the Mount then was to set these false commandments apart from the law, and then to enlarge the law to its fullest extent in preparation for the world-wide ministry of the apostles.

In v. 21, Jesus mentions the first of several half-truths[3] and whole perversions of the Old Testament: "You have heard that it was said to them of old time, you shall not murder; and whoever murders will be guilty in a law-court." Jesus indicates that the commandment meant much more than this. He proceeds to enumerate a number of attitudes which have the same moral quality as "murder," namely resentment or anger, and contempt or abuse. Notice that the traditional interpretation was quite limited: "murder" was subject to the jurisdiction of a local Jewish council. And beyond that the rabbis did not deign to go. But Jesus had no such self-imposed limitations. He came to fill in what the rabbis had left out! Hence Jesus argued that malice and the anger which grows out of it are also in danger of the local council (the lower court); but what the rabbis did not even consider, calling a man by some contemptuous name (today it might be "kike," "polack," "square," "pig"), should be a matter for the whole Sanhedrin (the Supreme Court of the land)! And, still more devastating of the Pharisees' superficial attitude in moral things, calling a man a "fool" is a thing which renders people subject to hell itself.

We cannot conceive of ourselves committing cold-blooded murder. But we excuse and even justify resentment, anger, contempt, and abuse. Yet Jesus says He considers them murder.

". . . and ye know that no murderer has eternal life abiding in him" (1 John 3:15).

Part of our problem is that we have a restricted sense of hatred and, as we shall see below, of love. We think that hatred must be intense, bitter, and ugly. Actually it may be only a careless remark, an unthinking barb thrown out on the spur of the moment. Or it may be an attitude inherited from our parents, or borrowed from our culture. For example, our friends who live in countries south of the border are said to resent our calling ourselves "Americans," as though we had exclusive claim to the term. But aren't they Americans too? Similarly, Christians of other countries do not like to be called "natives," with all the overtones of savagery that word carries. These are little things, perhaps, but they are the things which separate, aggravate, and alienate people who should be in close communion.

Intensity is not of the essence of the act of hating. We hate what we "don't like."

In the verses which follow (vv. 23, 24) Jesus not only further applies the law against murder, but He also stresses that there is a definite connection between life and worship. He introduces the new paragraph with the words, "If therefore . . ." to indicate this connection. The commandment against "not liking people" applies to worship. Worship is part of man's obligation to God; in fact it is also his highest privilege but it must be done in a context of love for men (1 John 4:20, 21). Hence a man must examine his heart for the weed of hatred and straighten out his relations with other men before his worship will be acceptable to God.

If there is any command of Christ which is being flaunted today, it is this one. Surely this means that our churches are often *too full*. There is a sin of absenting one's self from church, but there is also a sin of going to church before Christ's command has been obeyed. We have social tensions, denominational tension, bickering over the preeminence of God's gifts, and the like. And yet we would not think of missing morning worship!

The Artificial Fruit to Be Detected

But we have not yet come to grips with the modern violations of this sin of "murder." To this subject Jesus returns in Matthew 5:43-45:

> You have heard that it was said, You shall love your neighbor, and hate your enemy: but I say to you, Love your enemies, and pray for them that persecute you; so that you may be the sons of your Father who is in heaven . . . .

The Pharisees had a very restricted view of who their neighbors were, and so they could easily infer that their enemies could be hated. This was not God's law (cf. Ex. 23:4, 5; Prov. 25:21f), and Jesus does not allow the perversion to pass. God does not countenance a limited love, for that is an artificial fruit, a Satanic counterfeit which frequently masquerades as the real thing.

With real irony, he compares what we are accustomed to call "sweet fellowship" (greeting one another cordially) with the gatherings of those most contemptible of fellows, the publicans. (Actually we may miss the effect of what Jesus is saying because it is difficult to have the same feeling toward the publicans as Jesus' hearers did. Some highly emotive word must be substituted in our thinking: for some, the word "commie" will conjure up the sort of feeling Jesus intended; for others, "establishment" may have the same effect.) At any rate publicans can have sweet fellowship too! That does not take grace. What takes grace is "to pray for them that persecute you" (v. 44), to give your enemy food and water (Prov. 25:21f).

I suspect there are not many Christians today earnestly pleading with God for the salvation of "commies," or "black militants." We may pray that God will "straighten them out" (with the implied thought that of course we do not need straightening out). Yet, what is needed more than anything else in this sin-divided world today is just what Jesus calls for here: the weeding out of that limited love which is making us smug, complacent and self-satisfied, and farther and farther removed from those who should see, not just what the publicans can produce, but what the Holy Spirit can produce, viz., love for our enemies.

These are the weeds and the artificial fruit which must be rooted out of all of us. In principle, Christians "have crucified the flesh with the affections and lusts" (Gal. 5:24), but there is a day-by-day process by means of which we should overcome these evil tendencies lest we devour one another (cf. Gal. 5:15, 26).

The Fruit to Be Cultivated

The Bible does not try to define "love."[4] It illustrates it. Nor do the Scriptures find grades or degrees of love, as we hear today of *eros*, "sensual love"; *philia*, "human love"; *agape*, "divine love." Although the Bible uses different Hebrew and Greek words, it uses them quite indiscriminately so that the word used for love for God also occurs in reference to human relationships. This should perhaps teach us that life cannot be easily pigeonholed, or too readily sliced up. All of life is love for God.

Leviticus 19:9-18 is an extended series of illustrations of what love is. The closing verses of this paragraph are the familiar words quoted by Jesus in Matthew 22:39 as the second "great commandment in the law" — "you shall love your neighbor as yourself." These words (Lev. 19:18b) seem to summarize the whole preceding paragraph, and it may be assumed that each of the commands mentioned in vv. 9-18 deals with a different aspect of love.

Before proceeding to a study of these aspects, we should notice a sentence which occurs no less than five times in the paragraph: "I am the Lord." The repetition can only serve to stress the importance of what is being said, and to emphasize the solemnity with which we are to receive it. If ever there were commandments which the Lord Himself took seriously, these are some of them!

In using the covenant Name we sometimes pronounce as "Jehovah," the Lord reminds us of two of the aspects of a covenantal relationship. As the sovereign of the covenant who graciously redeems His servants and restores them to righteousness, God is here reminding the Israelites to do to others what He Himself has done to them. But on the other hand, the sovereign lays down the covenant's sanctions. It is a fearful thing to violate the covenant of the living God. The fact that this is repeated again and again indicates the priority God places on love for other human beings.

1. *Concern for the Poor*

> And when you reap the harvest of your land, do not wholly reap the corners of your field, nor gather the gleanings of your harvest. Do not glean your vineyard, nor gather every grape of your vineyard; but leave them for the poor and stranger: I am the Lord your God (Lev. 19:9, 10).

Deuteronomy 24:19-21 enlarges on what is said here. The Israelite farmer must deliberately leave grain and grapes for the poor and the stranger.

The concern which the Jewish community, and later the Christian church, should have for the poor — this is a study which needs to be undertaken in our day. For our purposes it should be stated that one reason affixed by God to this commandment is, "You shall remember that you were a slave in Egypt" (Deut. 24:22). Thus concern for the poor is not, for the Christians, mere philanthropy, or a dole, or a tax exemption. It is a moral responsibility, a desire to share what one has received because God has been gracious to us. If we remember our "Egypt," we shall easily remember the poor.

But perhaps another reason should be mentioned. What we have, we have *by grace*. But also, what we have, we have *as stewards*. David recalled this truth in words we often quote at offering time, "All things are from you, and of your own we have given you" (1 Chron. 29:14). We have a concern for the poor because we have in our hands some of God's wealth and He has commanded us to distribute it abundantly. This is the biblical corrective to an excessive and perverted emphasis on private ownership. The Christian has his private wealth so that he may give it away to those who are in need (Eph. 4:28).

And lest we fear to be abundant givers, God has decreed a law which would probably baffle secular economists: "He who has gathered much has nothing over; and he who had gathered little had no lack . . . . this I say, he who sows sparingly shall reap also sparingly; and he who sows bountifully shall reap also bountifully" (2 Cor. 8:15; 9:6).

The fact that modern governments are usurping this function as givers to the poor should not encourage us to think that we are thus relieved of this responsibility. It is still *an essential part of Christian living*, important enough for the "pillars" and Paul to mention in their conference of Galatians 2:10.

Contemporary Christian groups will have to use their ingenuity and sanctified imagination to implement this command.[5] It is passing strange, in view of what both Testaments say about caring for the poor, that some men will call helping the poor a "social gospel." There is a vast difference between the social demands of the gospel message and the so-called social gospel. The latter is a ministry based on a denial of the Scripture's teaching regarding sin, and the necessity for a Redeemer. But the Scriptures teach those who have been redeemed to have a care for men's needs, and frequently this care must begin with seeing that they have enough to eat.

Moreover, it is odd that men shy away from this commandment on the pretext that Jesus' words, "You have the poor with you always" (Mark 14:7), only indicate that poverty will never be eradicated from human living, and hence we should have no concern for men's bodies. The answer lies in finishing the verse: "and whenever you want to, you may do them good." Jesus is here echoing the words of Deuteronomy 15:11, "For the poor will never cease out of the land: therefore I command you, saying, Open your hand wide to your brother, to your poor, and to the needy in your land."

2. *Integrity in Business Transactions*

> Do not steal, nor deal falsely, nor lie one to another (Lev. 19:11).

Most of us have no idea how holy God is, or how holy He expects us to be. Bonar comments on this passage: "There is a contamination of conscience too frequently found in even Christian men, from continual intercourse with an unconscientious world. Glorify God, therefore, by a jealous integrity, and by a noble uprightness."[6]

The "noble uprightness" is spelled out for us in a passage like Leviticus 6:2ff. Moses here mentions a few cases in which an Israelite might trespass against his neighbor: (1) a neighbor might ask him to keep something for him while he is away and then the whole thing is forgotten — by default the Israelite gains possession of it; (2) the Israelite and his neighbor might enter into a transaction based on the neighbor's acceptance of the Israelite's word, the latter having not been entirely forthright; (3) the Israelite might take advantage of his neighbor's hardship, as Jacob did of Esau's (Gen. 25:29ff); (4) he might use brute strength, as Naboth did (1 Kings 21:2ff); (5) he might find something which was lost and lie about finding it, or else make no effort to return it to his neighbor. All of these are acceptable business tactics in a world which makes might right, but in any of these things an Israelite would have committed a trespass; he would have had to make restitution to the neighbor he had defrauded; and then he would have been required to bring a trespass-offering because his sin against his neighbor was also a trespass of God's law.

We must bring these instances up-to-date. This law calls for total integrity in selling our car or our house; in dealing with those who work for us, or who are our students. It is a complete reversal of the old rhyme — "Finders keepers, losers weepers."

A number of years ago, a shopkeeper gave me change for five dollars even though I had given her only one dollar to pay for my purchase. When I called this to her attention, she exclaimed, "You're sure going to heaven." I confessed to her that I was, but added, "Not the way you think." She was surprised at ordinary honesty, but this should be commonplace to the Christian. It is called for by God's law and the motivation for it is Christian love.

3. *The Sanctity of God's Name*

> Do not swear by my name falsely, and do not profane the name of your God: I am the Lord" (Lev. 19:12).

Israelites did not have many written documents to record their agreements and contracts. They resorted to oral statements, and, when the situation required, oaths and vows. In particular, when a man would say, "God is my witness," or, "As the Lord lives," or, "The Lord do so to me and more. . . ." this was the end of all discussion. The sacred Name had been invoked and it was unthinkable that anyone could do that and still deceive his neighbor: "For the Lord will not hold him guiltless who takes his name in vain."

But to use the Name to defraud was also a transgression against the law of love to one's neighbor. Hence it is included here among other such commandments.

Contemporary Christians are not apt to use God's Name as an idle oath. But blasphemy rears its head in another subtle and insidious way. Frequently we hear people announcing a certain course of action and then justifying it by saying, "I (think, or feel, or know) that it is the Lord's will." Sometimes it turns out all right, but just as frequently it seems to work out otherwise. The Name had been used to justify our desires or our reasoning but it has been used vainly.

And this also is a transgression against our neighbor. For who of us would dare to suggest another course of action when it has been confidently declared, "This is the Lord's will." We are then barred from helping our neighbor with good advice, or at least from a profitable discussion with him as to the wisdom of his intended course. We are called upon to bear one another's burdens, but how may we do this when "the Lord's will" effectively prohibits this?

4. *Prompt Payment of Wages*

> Do not defraud your neighbor, and don't rob him: the wages of the man who works for you should not abide with you all night until the morning (Lev. 19:13).

Our economy today is based on a payday which is mutually acceptable to both management and labor. In formal business operations, such obligations are met on time. But what about informal arrangements? Moses insists that, in keeping with the commercial arrangements of his time, a man be paid at the end of each working day. James 5:4 deals with a similar situation some 1500 years later.

The point is that we should love men enough not to make life hard for them, so we should go out of our way to pay our debts (especially our informal ones) and be careful to keep our word with respect to them.

This commandment bears on many situations in Christian circles today. When a church is slow to pay its commitment to a missionary, it should remember that the missionary might be going without. When a visiting minister has to wait months for his traveling expenses, he might have to make a loan to meet his expenses. When an institution falls behind three or four months in its salaries, life can be hard for those who are on the payroll.

This principle is not meant to apply to cases where funds may not be available. Moses speaks of not allowing the wages to stay in the employer's pocket; in other words, in the case before us the funds are available. And when they are available, God's law and the law of love demand that they be paid.

Uncritical apologists for capitalism do not distinguish adequately between private ownership, which has biblical sanction, and the private motive, which can be a euphemism for greed and lust. The economics of the Old Testament was so structured that the great wealth of the Promised Land was shared by all the people. Lands, if taken from their owners to satisfy debts, were returned to them at the end of seven years and in the year of Jubilee. If a man enslaved himself to repay a debt, he was granted his liberty at the same intervals.[7]

These customs recognize the validity of debts and the necessity for paying them. But they also prevent the great amassing of riches. (In Isaiah's day, Shebna the treasurer did grow rich, but for this he was punished severely, cf. ch. 22:15-19.)

The Proverbs praise the provident man who saves so that he will not be dependent on others, and rebukes the slothful man who will not work, but the laws of the Old Testament required such recognition of the poor that no man could become rich at the expense of others.

Paul states the matter bluntly in Ephesians 4:28, where he gives a proper reason for saving money — that a man "may have whereof to give to him who has need."

When men argue that Christianity and capitalism are related, they should tell the whole story. Jesus warned against trusting in riches; in fact, He spoke of the difficulty of having a rich man come to Him (Luke 12:13ff; 18:24). Paul cautioned the rich people in the church not to be "high-minded, nor have their hope set on the uncertainty of riches, but on God who gives us richly all things to enjoy; that they be ready to distribute, willing to communicate; laying up for themselves a good foundation against the time to come, that they may lay hold on the life which is life indeed" (1 Tim. 6:17ff). A little earlier in the chapter he had written: "They that are minded to be rich fall into temptation and a snare and many foolish and hurtful lusts, such as drown men in destruction and perdition. For the love of money is a root of all kinds of evil: which some reaching after have been led astray from the faith, and have pierced themselves through with many sorrows" (vv. 9, 10).

5. *Care for the Less Privileged*

> Do not curse the deaf, nor put a stumbling block before the blind, but fear your God: I am the Lord (Lev. 19:14).

Most of us would be shocked if there were a literal infraction of this command, but it must have been a problem in Moses' time else he would not have mentioned it here. On

Mount Ebal the nation was required to pronounce a curse on such a deed (Deut. 27:18). David felt that he had been mistreated in some fashion as this (Ps. 38:13-17).

But it is the spirit of the act which should be uppermost in our minds, and it is probably to this that Jesus alludes in Matthew 5 (cf. p. 46 above) when he rebukes us for calling a man, "Fool." Even if we shrink from this, we can still enjoy it when a choir member of dubious musical talent misses a note, or when someone who has missed out in social graces commits a *faux pas*, or when an awkward athlete looks silly in a losing cause. The commandment is not against laughing *with* a competent performer who makes the mistake we all do; the command forbids laughing *at* the person, lacking in the ordinary advantages and abilities of life, who makes a public display of himself.

6. *Respect of Persons*

> Don't be unrighteous in judgment: do not respect the person of the poor, nor honor the person of the mighty: but in righteousness judge your neighbor (Lev. 19:15).

The Lord is giving us examples of love. The world is bright and fair to the man who has money, fame, and health, but is a cold and cruel place indeed to the poor and unknown. It was not to be so in Israel. But James found it so in the early church. When rich or famous men came into their assemblies, the Christians fawned all over them, gave them more than they needed, and generally forgot the evils which rich men commit. But the poor were ignored, or degraded.

James is quite forthright about it all. "If you have respect to persons, you commit sin, and are convicted by the law as transgressors" (2:9).

Ministers of the Gospel receive this sort of treatment today, but while they are enjoying the compliments which they do not need, many a needy person walks quietly from the church with a feeling of emptiness in his heart when one word of kindness would have made the whole week ahead bright and cheery.

But the force of the commandment lies much deeper than

just disapproving of favoritism. Moses and James have called us to "righteous judgment." That is, we should form our opinions and make our judgments after hearing two sides of any issue. Dr. Howard A. Kelly once adapted a statement of the Roman philosopher Seneca: *audi et alteram partem* ("Hear also the other side"; Dr. Kelly added the "also"). He said, "You may have judged truly but you have not judged righteously until you have heard also the other side." The Bible turns us from people to the evidence in making judgments. In the context of Leviticus 19, this is not only righteousness, it is also true love.

7. *Integrity in Speech*

> Do not go up and down as a talebearer among your people: do not stand against the blood of your neighbor: I am the Lord (Lev. 19:16).

Ezekiel had a message for the "bloody city" of Jerusalem (ch. 22). He was to show her all her abominations: she was shedding blood, worshiping idols, dishonoring parents and orphans, profaning Sabbaths, and oppressing strangers. In v. 9 he noted that there were men there who carry tales to shed blood. This was contrary to God's law as it is recorded here in Leviticus. The Lord undoubtedly has physical murder in mind here and he warns about such tale-telling as would destroy one's neighbor. This is not a sin which might be prevalent in our churches today.

But the sin of character assassination, or of loose talking which leads to the discrediting of an individual is widespread in Christian circles, so much so that in church disputes it is frequently difficult to get at the truth of a matter. Loose talking should be countered by a scrupulous concern for the truth and for the sacred name of the person. Whether we like him or not, whether he is on our "side" or not, he bears the image of God and his name and reputation are worth preserving.

John (in 21:20ff) tells a story which might be humorous if it weren't so serious. Jesus had just told Peter how he would die. Peter, naturally enough, was curious about the manner of

John's death, but Jesus put him off: "If I desire that he stay till I return, what is that to you? Follow me." Now notice the talebearing of the saints! "Then this saying went abroad among the brethren that that disciple would not die. But Jesus did not say to him, He will not die; but, If I desire that he should stay until I return, what is that to you?"

The saints' story was a bit more spectacular than the one Jesus told. What they said might have seemed "logical" to them. But it was not what Jesus said, and John sought to correct it. Probably no harm was done to John's person because of this talebearing, but there are many instances where similar carelessness with the truth has brought shame and lasting discredit. This sort of talk is not in conformity with the law of love.[8]

8. *Open Criticism*

> Do not hate your brother in your heart; you shall surely rebuke your neighbor and not load sin upon yourselves because of him (Lev. 19:17).

Psychologists today tell us how much harm is done to us when we bottle up our feelings. The Lord here is speaking, not of damage which might be done to our personalities, but of guilt which attaches itself to secret hatred — guilt and hatred which might be avoided if we openly criticized and thus helped one another. It should be noted that this command comes in a context of brotherly love. Such concern dictates that one should let his brother know how he feels toward him. (In passing it should be noted that "brother" and "neighbor" are synonyms. In a Christian context a neighbor is a brother, and a brother is a neighbor.)

Why should love dictate criticism? Look at the number of broken friendships, ruptured fellowships, because one person has criticized another! But we must look a little deeper. An uncriticized man is one who will pursue his course ignorant of consequences unless someone who can see what he cannot see tells him of his peril. Is it better to lose his friendship and deliver his soul, or keep his friendship by silence and thus aid and abet his failure and loss?

But is this the only option open to a neighbor? The Israelites were the people of God. They had been brought out of Egypt, "the house of bondage." They had been helpless, ignorant slaves. Whatever they had now was theirs because of the grace of God. They had no reputation to protect; they should not be threatened by some revelation of their weakness or waywardness. Everyone knew what his brother had been and would be. It was all out in the open!

It is so with Christians today. We have been brought out of the horrible pit (or so we like to testify) and out of the miry clay (as least we sing about it), then why are we edgy, threatened, or even insulted when someone (friend or foe) tells us that some of the clay still clings to us? Whom are we kidding when we act as if we had not been in sin, and still act as sinners?

It is interesting to note how in the Scriptures a Christian was identified by what he had been before his conversion. Simon, *the leper* (Matt. 26:6), Mary Magdalene, *out of whom Jesus had cast seven devils* (Luke 8:2), Matthew, *the publican* (Matt. 10:3). Moreover in Ephesians 4:28, Paul can say quite openly, "Let him that stole steal no more." The Ephesians knew about whom Paul was speaking. The past lives of the saints were an open book.

But criticism is not a one-way street. Rebukes might be received in humility and love; they also must be given in humility and love. What is the difference morally between the rebuker and the rebuked? Later on in the Galatian letter, Paul speaks of the "spiritual" restoring the offender "in a spirit of meekness, considering yourself, lest you also be tempted." Such bearing of burdens fulfills this law.

Our churches will be healthier when we "confess our faults one to another," and when we "surely rebuke our neighbor."

9. *Disposition to Bless*

> You shall not avenge or [following Delitzsch] cherish a design against your fellow-countrymen (Lev. 19:18).

Says Charles Hodge, "It is peculiarly characteristic of the

spirit of the gospel that it turns the heart towards others, and away from their own interests. Self is not the Christian's centre; men are loved because they are men, Christians because they are Christians; the former with sincere sympathy and benevolence, the latter with brotherly affection. The happiness and feelings of others, the gospel teaches us to consult in small, as well as in great matters, *anticipating each other in all acts of kindness and attention* [italics ours] . . . Just so far, therefore, as we find our hearts indisposed to bless those who curse us, or inclined to indulge even a secret satisfaction when evil comes upon them, are we unchristian in our temper."[9]

The Means to Cultivate This Fruit

Physical fruit grows because it is produced by a living plant; it may even grow when it is unattended. The analogy for the Christian life cannot be pressed. The Christian is a new creature, a branch on the vine; yet he is responsible for taking an active part in the producing of fruit. The Bible knows nothing of wild fruit in the area of Christian sanctification.

The Scriptures, preeminently, are the means of grace to the child of God. Reflection upon, and obedience to the Word of truth brings Christian character and the fruit of the Spirit. But what, specifically, will nourish the love which we have seen God's law requires of us?

It cannot be overemphasized that for the Christian, love has already been given him. In the new birth he has already been "created after God," "he has been raised to newness of life." Hence sanctification is not imposing a new conduct on an individual, it is providing a climate, or an environment in which the newly planted seed will germinate and appear. This truth we have tried to stress in Chapter 2.

God has given us examples of His own love. We may note three passages from the New Testament, one of which we have already studied. In Matthew 5:44ff, after Jesus had quoted the verse from Leviticus 19:18, He spoke of loving our enemies and then He gave His Father as the outstanding example of this. God's enemies enjoy sunshine and rain. If we want to be His children we must live as He does, and do good to all men. The next time we meet a particularly repulsive individual and all our self-righteousness wells up within us and we are ready to "vent our spleen," we should look up at the sun and the clouds and remember our Father's love. If we hear this word, we will begin to love.

In Ephesians 4:31, 32, Paul bids Christians to be kind to each other, and as an example he holds up the forgiveness of Christ, which is the foundation of all our hope. If Christ would treat us as we are tempted to treat others, where would any of us be?

I would like to have been in Colosse, in the house of Philemon, when Onesimus arrived bearing Paul's note. Before reading the letter, Philemon probably remembered how useless Onesimus had been, how much he had wronged him. Anticipating Philemon's first reaction, Paul in the letter draws his attention to the enormous debt Philemon owes to Paul: "lest I should mention that you owe to me even your own self as well." When Philemon reflected on all that Jesus had done for him, to do kindness to Onesimus as a brother was a very small thing. This is why I said above that the means to cultivate love are the experiences we have of responding to His own love to us.

Questions for Chapter 5

1. In Galatians 5:14 Paul says, "All the law is fulfilled in one word, in the statement, You shall love your neighbor as yourself." By a study of Old Testament law, moral, civil and ceremonial, show that this is true.
2. Why is love such a rare thing in the world and in the church? What causes hatred? Study First John 3:11, 12 in this connection.
3. In what areas of life should Christian groups develop a loving attitude today? How can Christians show more love to each other?

4. How can our love be made practical in, e.g., labor-management relations, race relations, in international politics? Should this be our aim?
5. Do you think love is greater than any of the other fruit?

Notes

[1] Cf. esp. vv. 13-15, 26–6:10.

[2] So I understand "fulfill" in Matt. 5:17. Cf. Murray, *Principles of Conduct,* p. 149f.

[3] For lengthy consideration of these verses, the reader is referred to Dr. Martyn Lloyd-Jones' two volumes, *Studies in the Sermon on the Mount,* and Murray, *op. cit.*, p. 159ff.

[4] E. D. Burton in *A Critical and Exegetical Commentary on The Epistle to the Galatians*, p. 521 suggests that "love" includes "the element of appreciation, recognition of worth, (but) . . . evidently lays chief stress upon the desire and will to benefit, which issues in efforts for the well-being of another."

[5] Cf. Appendix, esp. C. F. H. Henry, *Aspects of Christian Social Ethics*, and W. L. Muncy, *Trustees of Creation*.

[6] Andrew Bonar, *A Commentary on the Book of Leviticus,* p. 348.

[7] Cf. Appendix, esp. Oehler.

[8] Years ago, in a board meeting, someone's name came up for discussion. "Oh," said one, "he is either muddle-headed or a liar." To defend the absent one another said, "Well, he may be muddle-headed but he certainly is no liar." The conversation was reported to the man who had been the topic of conversation, but only a part of what had been said: "So-and-so said you're muddle-headed." Thus was created a misunderstanding which to my knowledge has never been corrected.

[9] *Commentary on the Epistle to the Romans*, p. 403f.

Chapter 6

Joy

SINCE WE CANNOT EMBRACE both Paul's Gospel and Judaizing teaching at the same time, it follows that we cannot have both joy and backbiting at once, for joy comes from grace, and backbiting is a result of dependence on works. Paul calls attention to these two traits of character, so that the Galatians might understand the choice which lay before them. But once again, Paul says nothing new. The Galatians might have learned this from the Old Testament.

The God of the Bible can sometimes be a gad-fly; He does not like to see people getting into a rut, and in His providence from time to time He turns things upside-down to shake them out of complacency. One of these times, in ancient Israel at least, was the annual Feast of Tabernacles.

"Tabernacles" is not the best word; "lean-to" which Boy Scouts sometimes make, would be a far better word. Here is the command as Moses gave it: "On the fifteenth day of the seventh month, when you have gathered in the fruits of the land . . . you shall take on the first day the fruit of goodly trees, branches of palm-trees, and boughs of thick trees, and willows of the brook . . . You shall dwell in lean-tos seven days . . . that your generation may know that I made the children of Israel to dwell in lean-tos, when I brought them out of Egypt'' (Lev. 23:39ff). ''And you shall rejoice in your feast'' (Deut. 16:14).

It seems ironic that the Lord would call for this feast just after the harvest when the Israelites were most aware of their wealth and most ready for a time of leisure after the hard labor of harvesting. They were to forsake whatever comforts they had, live in primitive conditions, and rejoice! Whatever else this privation accomplished it separated those who had a deep-seated joy from those whose happiness depended on outward circumstances; and it taught the whole congregation that ''a man's life does not consist in the abundance of the things which he possesses.''

The farmer who is weeding his garden, when he comes to the fruit, joy, has to be especially careful because not all joy is good fruit, not all sorrow is rank weed. He must become expert in separating weeds and fruit. God, the master Gardener, has an effective way of distinguishing them; in His providence He directs circumstances which strip away all temporal props, so that true joy may be seen in its simplicity.

Not all sorrow is antithetic to joy. In fact, some sorrow is conducive to it. In this sinful world, sorrow has a work to do, and when that is over, joy appears.

But there is a sorrow which is sin, and another sorrow which is the result of sin. These are the weeds in the gardens of many men's souls.

The Weeds to Be Rooted Out

Paul speaks of the sorrow which comes from hopelessness facing death (1 Thess. 4:13), the sorrow of the world (2 Cor. 7:10); Hebrews mentions the sorrow of unrepentant Esau (cf. 12:16). This sorrow is rebellion against the providence of God, against the just punishment which is the consequence of sin; it is the sorrow of ''being caught.'' Because the person who is guilty of this sorrow is selfish and seeks for all his spiritual resources within himself, he is hopeless and compounds his sinfulness by preferring the sorrow of hopelessness to the gracious provision of God.

Thus the weed differs from godly sorrow, not in its intensity, but in its motivation. The sorrow of the world reveals a frustrated ego; godly sorrow repents of a rebellion against a holy God.

All of us Christians may indulge this weed from time to time but sooner or later we see it for what it is and turn to the Lord for forgiveness and comfort. But the weed frequently appears as self-pity and then it is more difficult to identify. Self-pity rears its head when we think that God no longer pities us. Such was the case of Elijah[1] when he heard that Jezebel had designs on his life. Even though he had been an object of the most direct supernatural care (the lack of rain because he requested it; the feeding by the ravens for a whole year; his support in the home of the widow who hid him; the immediate answer to his prayer for fire, and then a bit later for rain), Elijah fell into self-pity because he did not see immediate and visible results of his ministry: "Enough now; take, Lord, my life, for I am not better than my fathers."

It would be idle to minimize Elijah's peril as he fled from Jezebel, but we must note that Elijah minimized his blessings. When he insisted that "I, only I, am left," his self-pity was surely distorting the facts. "Because Elijah had not seen the expected salutary results of his zeal for the Lord, he thought that all was lost, and in his gloomy state of mind overlooked what he had seen a short time before with his own eyes, that even in the neighborhood of the king himself there lived a pious and faithful worshipper of Jehovah, viz. Obadiah, who had concealed a hundred prophets from the revenge of Jezebel, and that the whole of the people assembled upon Carmel had given glory to the Lord, and at his command had seized the prophets of Baal and put them to death, and therefore the true worshippers of the Lord could not all have vanished out of Israel."[2]

Elijah's self-pity, like all self-pity, grew out of a faulty basis for security and joy. He wanted to find happiness in success, but even success in the Lord's work is a broken reed if we lean on it for security. Moreover, because he was looking in the wrong place for a prop for his well-being, Elijah was blinded to what was really going on.

A closer study of the passage will reveal this and should serve to sustain us when we are tempted to self-pity. Elijah took off from the city of Jezreel and went south to Beer-sheba, that is, out of the jurisdiction of Jezebel, and then proceeded into the desert another day's journey. There he was met by an angel and was fed twice "because the journey is too great for you." Then, in the strength of that food, he proceeded to wander about in the desert (from Beer-sheba to Horeb is about two hundred miles) for forty days. The coincidence of the number of days corresponding to the years of Israel's wandering must have reminded him of God's care for the nation in the years past, and the fact that he was sustained for so long a time by food provided by the angel could only have reminded him of the water and the manna.

Finally at Horeb the Lord reminded him again of Moses, who at that very spot had seen God in the wind, the earthquake, and the fire. *But God was not in these in Elijah's time.* Now God spoke in "a soft, gentle rustling" (so Keil).

God does not always work as we want Him to — God does not have to work as we want Him to. Our source of joy must be God, not His ways of working. Because Elijah insisted on a certain fixed pattern of operation, he fell into sorrow and despair. Elijah's search for joy in the wrong place led to blindness, which then bore him selfishness, callousness, and despair. Such is the weed of worldly sorrow as it masquerades in self-pity.

But worldly sorrow appears in yet another form. We claim as a birthright the privilege of "griping," or "murmuring" to use the language of the King James Version. We see it at its worst in the continuous attitude of complaining among the Israelites, and Paul speaks of the heinousness of it in 1 Corinthians 10:10.

The Lord had a clear understanding of what He was doing when He led the Israelites out of Egypt. He was saving them from bondage, and preparing them to be a nation of priests for the sake of the rest of the world. On the contrary, the Israelites seemed never to have gotten the point. On the basis of a false understanding of their election, they constantly murmured against the Lord their Savior. In their minds His love was turned into hate: "Because the Lord hated us, he has brought us forth out of the land of Egypt, to deliver us into the hand of the Amorites, to destroy us" (Deut. 1:27). They often treated God as though He were no better than a man; so the Scriptures say that they "tempted" Him (Ex. 17:2), probably indicating that the people almost dared God to do something evil to them. When the whole congregation murmured against Moses and Aaron (Num. 14:11), the Lord said they were "scorning" Him.

As the Israelites saw it, the problem was that God was not living up to His promises. Actually, they did not pay attention to His promises. If they had done so, they might have agreed with Joshua who said, " . . . you know in all your hearts and in all your souls, that not one thing has failed of all the good things which the Lord your God spoke concerning you; all have come to pass for you, and not one thing has failed" (Josh. 23:14).

Now disregarding God's promises is nothing more nor less than unbelief. And murmuring is unbelief and stems from unbelief. Note the contrast between "murmuring" and "faith." In Numbers 14:11, God asks, ". . . how long will it be before they believe me?" The Psalmist, describing their murmuring, wrote: " . . . they hearkened not to the voice of the Lord" (Ps. 106:25). Isaiah predicted a day when " . . . they that murmured shall learn doctrine" (29:24, where the Septuagint reads, "shall obey").

It is right here that the line between legitimate criticism and murmuring appears. The former is a discontent born of faith and proceeds on the basis of the promises of God; it is positive in its outlook and wholesome in its effect. Paul was certainly not content with the Galatians' plight, nor was Luther satisfied with conditions in the Romish church. They both claimed better things for the church of God. But murmuring is rebellious ignoring of the prerogatives of God; it is negative in its outlook and, in the end, utterly destructive of all good.

There is one more weed, a particularly noxious one, which calls for attention. In John 16:20, Jesus speaks of the joy of the world at His "leaving." We may recall the sense of "good riddance" in Pilate's mind when Jesus was led away; of Judas' feeling of elation when first he received the money; of the pleasure experienced by the rulers when they saw that the throng was following their lead. This was joy, but it was a diabolical sort of thing, akin to the shrieks of demons when Eve reached for the fruit. This is a joy born of hatred and unbelief.

There is a certain exhilaration in sin, especially when the sinner feels that he has called God's bluff and has gotten away with it. The Russian cosmonauts seemed pleased to relay back to earth that they saw no evidence for God as they made their first several orbits about our planet. Their satisfaction lay in the belief that their atheism had been confirmed. But anyone can have this sort of satisfaction during some time in his life. It is especially important that every child of God see this weed for what it is and not be enticed by it.

The Artificial Fruit to Be Detected

While the Bible recognizes that sinners have fun (Heb. 11:25), it insists that it will not last long. But what many people do not recognize is that saints frequently enjoy an artificial fruit which is of equally short duration. The experience is positive; it is born of wholesome circumstances; but Jesus warns against it.

He had sent the seventy out to witness, and they returned flushed with success. "Lord, even the demons are subject to us in your name" (Luke 10:17). Jesus reminded them that this was so, and that even greater things would be done by them in His power. But He went on, "Nevertheless in this rejoice not, that the spirits are subject to you; but rejoice that your names are written in heaven." Jesus words may perhaps carry greater force if we note the significance of the present tense in the original — "Do not continually rejoice that demons are subject to you, but rejoice continuously that your names stand written in the heavens."

Jesus knew what lay ahead for the disciples. There would be lean years, and unless their joy was based on eternal truths they would soon be sad indeed. This is not to suggest that we should not rejoice over blessings; the point is, we should not rejoice too much and make blessings more significant to us than the Giver of those blessings.

The Fruit to Be Cultivated

Love and faith have many children, and since many of our children are dissimilar even though they are offspring of the same parents, so too godly sorrow and godly joy are members of the same family. Paul said, "Rejoice with them that rejoice; weep with them that weep" (Rom. 12:15).

The Bible has many instances of godly sorrow. The saints wept when they understood that they would not see Paul again in this life (Acts 20:38); Paul felt that he had been delivered from sorrow when Epaphroditus was healed (Phil. 2:27); the apostolic band knew daily sorrow (2 Cor. 6:10); and both Jesus and Paul wept when they thought of the obstinacy of unbelief (Luke 19:41; Rom. 9:2). James (4:9), in keeping with the Old Testament's call for broken hearts, told sinning saints to turn their joy into grief. Peter said that the Christians living in the world would always be subject to sorrows because of the treatment they would receive (1 Peter 2:19).

These instances, and there are many others, spring from a belief of the truth and from a love for God and for people. The world being what it is, the Christian who has been enlightened can only bear a heavy heart as he looks at sin and its ravages in the world.

But, at the same time, the Bible calls for joy as an abiding possession and a permanent state of mind for the saint. James 1:2 even suggests that temptation is a reason for rejoicing. Though Paul was in prison, he was glad for his imprisonment and for some of the vilification he was strangely receiving from those outside prison (Phil. 1:18). Both Paul and John express joy at hearing of growth in grace on the part of their converts (Phil. 1:5; 2:2; 4:10; 2 John 4). In fact, Paul seems to make a blanket command to be joyful under any and all occasions (Phil. 4:4; 1 Thess. 5:16).

Such joy has its origin in God. It is called joy "in" or "of" the Holy Spirit, and it is produced by faith (Rom. 14:17; 15:13). It is that state of mind which is induced by a believing reception of the truths of the Gospel and by being a part of that community which is made up of saints (1 John 1:4). It is not dependent on outward circumstances, but is based on the reality of God and of the immutability of His promises. It is not a pious front, a sort of sanctified "cheese" smile whenever we think people are watching us; it is the positive feeling of the whole man that God's will is being done. It was the feeling in Messiah's heart as He suffered for men: "I *delight* to do your will, O my God" (Ps. 40:8, italics mine).

It should be apparent from the foregoing that joy is more basic, more deep-seated than godly sorrow. John predicted a day when tears would be wiped away, and there would be no more pain. At that day, joy will be unmixed; meantime sorrow has a work to do, and part of its work is to make joy a reality in the Christian.

The Bible dwells on this relation of sorrow to joy in the believer. Jesus introduces us to the connection when He uses the example of the woman giving birth to the child. Soon she forgets her pains, intense though they have been, because a child has been born and the joy blots out the memory of the pain. But in this sinful world there are no births without birth-pangs. Similarly God has decreed that our entrance into glory be attended by a struggle with sin and its consequences. In fact, there is a kind of necessity about it all: ". . . through many tribulations we *must* enter the kingdom of God" (Acts 14:22; cf., also Rom. 8:17; 2 Thess. 1:4ff; 2 Tim. 2:12).

Paul speaks of a specific sort of sorrow which is the lot of every Christian. He had written a pretty sharp letter to the Corinthians and had made them unhappy. In fact Paul himself felt remorse at having to write as he did. Yet notice the happy outcome. The Corinthians repented, sorrowing after a godly manner, and both they and Paul could now rejoice at the outcome (cf. 2 Cor. 2:3f; 7:8f).

There is a kind of direct proportion between sorrow for sin and joy in the Holy Spirit. Those who feel the worst about their sins, feel the happiest about forgiveness. It is just at this point that some modern preaching robs Christians of their fullness of joy. Sin is soft-pedaled, and so then is the joy of salvation. Even in our hymnody changes have been made to cushion the effect of sin. Just to take one illustration, many of our modern hymnals read.

> The dying thief rejoiced to see
> That fountain in his day;
> And there may I, though vile as he,
> Wash all my sins away.

That word "though" puts the thief in his place. He was a bad man, worthy to die. But God's grace is so great that *even if I were as bad as he* I could still be forgiven. What nonsense! The original form of the hymn is much closer to Scripture: the third line reads, "And there may I *as* vile as he . . . ." But until we feel as vile as the thief, we shall not know the joy of the Lord!

Hebrews speaks of yet another sorrow-joy relationship. In chapter 12, we face the problem of chastening. Realistically the author reminds us that chastening is never a happy experience: it is not meant to be. Yet it yields happy results when we are exercised by it. That word "exercised" is the root from which we derive our word "gymnasium." Some suggest that a better translation is "trained." Chastening yields a fruit which makes for joy and peace when we are trained by it.

Here again we would all be happier if we took sin seriously. If we only knew how bad we are, we would welcome chastening because this is God's way of getting rid of sin and its habits. But chastening is resented because we cannot believe that we have done anything worthy of it.

Bernard seems to have expressed the thoughts of this chapter well:

Jesus, our only joy be Thou,
As Thou our prize wilt be;
Jesus, be Thou our glory now,
And through eternity.

The Means to Cultivate This Fruit

"Because you did not serve the Lord your God with joyfulness, and with gladness of heart, by reason of the abundance of all things; therefore you will serve your enemies . . . " (Deut. 28:47). One of the best means to induce joy into our lives is to see how much our heavenly Father hates ungodly sorrow. Moses predicts here that one of the chief causes of the Exile will be the lack of joy on the part of the Israelites. In other words, they will not learn the lesson of the Feast of Tabernacles but in their unbelief and disobedience will look to circumstances alone for the basis of their joy.

But a further reflection upon God's character will help us to rejoice despite outward conditions. William Cowper put it this way,

Sometimes a light surprises the Christian while he sings;
It is the Lord, who rises with healing in His wings:
When comforts are declining, He grants the soul again
A season of clear shining, to cheer it after rain.

Though vine nor fig-tree neither their wonted fruit shall bear,
Though all the field should wither, no flocks nor herds be there;
Yet God the same abiding, His praise shall tune my voice,
For, while in Him confiding, I cannot but rejoice.

Cowper, of course, was echoing the sentiments of Habakkuk. Who can be sorrowful while he is contemplating the wisdom, love, and power of God? This is why ungodly sorrow is so noxious a weed. It is practical atheism, for it ignores God and His attributes. If I believe that God is wise, then this circumstance will have a beneficial result for me. If He is loving, then it is inconceivable that He would allow it to happen if it will not work for good. If He is omnipotent, then no other power stronger than He has overcome Him and is now in control of the universe. Hence, in His wisdom and love, He is still in command.

"Rejoice in the Lord always, and again I say, rejoice."

Questions for Chapter 6

1. Is it possible to have joy and sorrow at the same time? Explain.
2. "The joy of the Lord is your strength" (Neh.8:10). Study the relation between strength and happiness. How much of our physical weakness, apathy, and illness is probably due to a heavy spirit?
3. Peter says that Christians have "joy inexpressible" as a present possession (1 Peter 1:8). What is the relation between distress (verse 6) and this joy? How can we experience something which is inexpressible?
4. What would make you happier than you are now?
5. How is joy related to the other fruit?

Notes

[1] Cf. 1 Kings 19.
[2] C. F. Keil, *The Books of the Kings*, p. 256.

Chapter 7

Peace

A RECENT VISITOR to Israel said that you cannot understand *shalom*[1] until you hear it spoken amid all the signs of war in Jerusalem. Only then does the deep sense of promise and of hope come through. This is probably true of most of the significant words in the Bible; we must be careful to understand them, as far as this is possible, in their ancient usage. We may well ask, has the modern Israeli captured the full biblical significance of the term?

In the Scriptures, *shalom* sometimes means little more than "hello," "good-by," "never mind." It can, more significantly, denote order, absence of strife, good health. Sometimes it is equivalent to "salvation," "reconciliation to God," and "heaven."

We cannot determine the meaning of "peace" until we see it in contrast to the several weeds which mar the garden of man's soul.

The Weeds to Be Rooted Out

1. *Anxiety*

"In nothing be anxious; but in everything by prayer and

supplication with thanksgiving let your requests be made known to God. And the peace of God, which passes all understanding, shall guard your hearts and thoughts in Christ Jesus" (Phil. 4:6, 7). Paul here is referring to the weed of anxiety, a sin which must be clearly distinguished from good and proper "care."

Anxiety is the preoccupation with things of lesser importance, in the false confidence that if they are well cared for, life will move smoothly along. Martha put more emphasis on cooking than on hearing Jesus talk. But she had her priorities mixed up. "Man does not live by bread alone, but by every word which proceeds out of God's mouth." The meal might go well, but what's a meal?

Similarly Jesus urged His disciples to understand what birds perceive instinctively. There are so many uncertainties in life, so many imponderables which are only in God's hand, that it is useless for us to set our minds on them. Worry is usurping God's prerogatives to give thought to food and clothing; or else it is a doubt that He cares about them. But in any case we must put emphasis on something which is within our power — the kingdom of God. "Is not life more than food?"

Care ceases to be anxiety when we bring God into the picture, when we "cast all our care upon Him" for then our priorities are in proper order. Anxiety is a weed because, like all other weeds, it is practical atheism. It counts some things more important than God and seeks to derive security from these things rather than from God Himself.

Anxiety may also beset the Christian who is intent on serving God, when his priorities are confused. John Bunyan's doubts and distresses were caused by his reading the Scriptures! But he chose to recall the threats of the law rather than the sweet promises of the Gospel and so fell into despair. When he heard the words of the Gospel at last, "Your righteousness is in heaven," and reflected on what that truth could mean to him, he found true peace with God. His doubts were in essence a denial of God's integrity because Bunyan chose to believe one part of the Scriptures to the exclusion of the other.

2. *Variance, Jealousy, Factions, Envyings*

These words are taken from the list of the works of the flesh in Galatians 5:20, 21. The ASV reads "strife, jealousy . . . factions . . . envyings."

a. The Greeks had a goddess *Eris* who excited people to war. The word *eris*, which I am translating "strife," also means "debate" or "contention." It comes from that restlessness of spirit which sees good in furor and has a delight in causing trouble.

The Proverbs have a word about this (6:16-19). "There are six things which the Lord hates, and seven are an abhorrence to his soul." As Delitzsch says, "The sense is not, that the six things are hateful to God, and the seventh an abomination to Him besides; . . . the seven are to be numbered separately, and the seventh is the *non plus ultra* of all that is hated by God."[2] This seventh is "sowing strife between brothers." Concerning this Delitzsch writes, "The chief of all that God hates is he who takes a fiendish delight in setting at variance men who stand nearly related."[3]

b. Jealousy (KJV reads "emulations") may be a virtue or an evil. So the word here translated "jealousy" may sometimes mean "zeal" in a good cause (John 2:17), and sometimes "envy" or "indignation" which has evil motivation.

As a work of the flesh, jealousy is that feeling of hatred which is produced in us when we see some good come to another; it may also become a desire to have for ourselves what another has. The Bible gives us two examples of this, one in a clearly carnal man, another in a saint. Ahab, when he discovered that he might not have Naboth's vineyard "came into his house heavy and displeased," lay down on his bed with his face to the wall, and would talk with no one nor eat. He evidently stayed there sulking while Jezebel did her dirty work. But when he heard that Naboth was dead, he arose and went down to see the vineyard. This is the weed of envy in all its heinousness. It has nothing to commend it; there is nothing attractive about it; even sinful Jezebel looked on him with contempt. But this is what happened to one man at least who had "sold himself to that which is evil in the sight of the Lord" (1 Kings 21:20).

Jealousy can be an incapacitating, debilitating, cancerous type of evil which causes a man to regress to childish attitudes and expressions. But jealousy more often spurs to action, to evil action, as we see in the case of David. We are accustomed to speaking of "David's sin," and by this we usually mean his adultery. Yet David's sin, as an exemplar for all the sins of man, was a multiple one. We see this especially in the way Nathan brings David to repentance. He does not mention the adultery, the deceit, the murder, nor even the lapse of time in which David lived with his guilt. All these were heinous enough. But Nathan concentrates on David's covetousness and envy, which were the hidden springs of all the other sins (2 Sam. 12:1-12).

c. What the KJV calls "strife" may probably best be represented as a base or low ambition which is concerned only with one's self. Perhaps also the gain intended is gross power or mere monetary gain.

Although this word is not used of him, the Diotrephes of Third John fits the definition. For a time at least he seems to have effectively opposed the apostle and those of whom the apostle approved. John says of him, "he wishes to be first," or "he likes to be the leader."[4] Diotrephes' ambition led him to evil speaking, to the breaking of fellowship and to excommunicating those who would not obey him. Clearly, this was a dictator who was stirring up the church because of his pride and ambition (3 John 9, 10).

3. *Peace Without God*

This is a weed which always leads to trouble — the determination to seek peace of any kind apart from God. Paul wrote, "Whenever they say, Peace and safety, at that time sudden destruction will come upon them" (1 Thess. 5:3). This happens, not because God is against peace, but He is a holy God and will grant peace only on the basis of righteousness.

Peace is essentially a gift of God, but men are required to seek it. And they must seek it intelligently. The false prophets of Jeremiah's day (indeed we find this as early as Micaiah) were preaching a false peace — a peace without God (Jer. 6:14). It became a slogan. The prophets of God developed a counter-slogan, "No peace," because men were making a god out of peace and were trying to heal "the hurt of the daughter of my people slightly" (v. 14). The last word might be translated "superficially"; Laetsch[5] suggests "carelessly."

Isaiah puts it bluntly — "there is no peace, says the Lord, to the wicked" (48:22).

The Artificial Fruit to Be Detected

There is a human characteristic which seems like peace, but it is downright sinful (carelessness), or pathological (apathy). What it amounts to is a denial of responsibility for what is going on in the world, or perhaps a disregard for God's majesty and a lack of involvement in things which concern Him.

The Gentiles of his day were "past feeling," says Paul in Ephesians 4:19. Sin had eroded their moral sense so that nothing alarmed them any longer. Such apathy was a sign of degeneracy, no matter how much it might appear outwardly as peaceful.

"Peace," as we shall see, is the companion of "life," but carelessness in doing one's duty is destructive to life. The artificial fruit should not be confused with the real thing.

The Fruit to Be Cultivated

It takes a troubled man to trouble a community; conversely peace will not come to a community until first of all it comes to the individual. Hence we should first speak of peace with God and peace with one's self, and then peace in a community.

1. *Individual Peace*

Isaiah said that there is no peace for the wicked. Paul is just as emphatic that there is peace to those who have been justified by faith in Jesus (Rom. 5:1). In the verses which follow Paul explains just what sort of peace he is talking about. In v. 9, he speaks about the wrath of God; in v. 10, he says there was a time when we were enemies. But all this has been changed now because Jesus has effected a reconciliation; this reconciliation takes the form of a justification through His blood; and Jesus' dying thus for us establishes for us the truth that God loves us.

What Paul puts in logical form, was played out for the Israelites in the peace-offering. Eating together, especially eating together in the other's home after there has been a disagreement, can be a token of reconciliation, that the breach of friendship has been mended. This truth God dramatized in the peace-offering, for after the animal had been killed and its blood sprinkled, the offerer and his family ate part of the carcass at the tabernacle as a symbol that there was peace between him and God. In similar fashion, the Lord's Supper, eaten in God's house, is a symbol of the peace that now obtains between a holy God and the sinner because of the reconciliation which was effected by the death of Jesus.

The first element in the peace which God gives, then, is the peace of friendship, of a breach removed, of a relationship restored. And when we remember that the relationship restored is between the eternal God and one of His creatures, and that this restoration was effected by God Himself in full conformity to the law, then this peace is seen to be complete, eternal, and sweet beyond comprehension.

Secondly, the peace which the redeemed individual enjoys is spiritually induced. It is not merely a psychological adjustment, or a sorting out of disturbing pressures to keep them in equilibrium. The Christian, as any human being, may have this sort of peace of mind. But Paul says[6] there is a peace which, to follow Lightfoot in his translation, surpasses "*every device or counsel of man,* i.e., which is far better, which produces a higher satisfaction, than all punctilious satisfaction, all anxious forethought."[7]

Now this peace, says Paul, shall "stand sentry" over your

hearts and minds, to protect them from all evil attacks. Peace with God does this because it is for all men the most fundamental relation. God promises that the man who has not made peace with Him will not be at peace with himself or with anyone else. He uses a most effective figure of speech in Isaiah 57:20f, "But the wicked are like the sea when it is tossed; for it cannot rest and its waters cast up slime and mud." Until this situation is remedied by divine grace, no man can escape from anxiety or from causing trouble.

Hence the peace mentioned in Philippians 4:6, 7 is a very broad term. It is almost a synonym for "salvation." In this sense, peace is complete. It is the "peace of peace," to use Isaiah's phrase in 26:3. Because it is complete, peace gives alacrity[8] to the redeemed individual because the great burden of sin has been removed (Eph. 6:15). It breeds confidence in us because we are assured that God is on our side completely, wholly. It is the confidence a man has when he realizes his wife is true to him; the confidence of a team when it knows the coach trusts it; the confidence of a missionary who knows he is supported by the promises of God and the prayers of his supporters. Such people are carefree in the best sense of that term.

So all-inclusive is the meaning of "peace" in the Scriptures that when God sets out to accomplish some of His greatest works, He is described as the *God of peace*: "The God of peace will bruise Satan under your feet shortly" (Rom. 16:20); "The God of peace will sanctify you wholly" (1 Thess. 5:23); "The God of peace, who brought again from the dead . . . our Lord Jesus" (Heb. 13:20).

2. *Communal Peace*

But God also gives peace to the Christian community. Paul reminds the Corinthians that there need be no confusion in worship services because God is the Author of peace (1 Cor. 14:33). The prophets and the tongues-speakers could not excuse their excesses in the Corinthian assembly on the ground that God was leading them!

But communal peace is to be seen not only in the context of

public worship; it governs and stands sentry over the whole life of the body of Christ. There is a bond of peace which guards the inner fellowship of the saints, and the peace makes itself evident in unity (Eph. 4:3). It makes it possible for God's people to live together peaceably. If each individual has peace with God, then his soul has been delivered from the restlessness which can cause strife; then having received the promise of good things from God, he can rejoice in the good which comes to another; if the peace of God is humbling him, then he sees the folly of self-assertiveness. Here we see peace as the weed-killer of envy, strife, and contention. But it is also fruit of the Spirit!

The peace of God goes even deeper. It "arbitrates" among believers (Col. 3:15). Lightfoot comments on this verse: "Whenever there is a conflict of motives or impulses or reasons, the peace of Christ must step in and decide which is to prevail."[9] He adds that the figure here is not one of power but of a decision to be made. In other words, whenever we have a difference of opinion, we should settle our differences so that peace is maintained and preserved. But we must hasten to add that it is "Christ's peace" which thus acts as umpire. We cannot render a decision in favor of false doctrine or of immorality on the ground that it will preserve peace. Righteousness and peace go together (cf. Ps. 85:10; Isa. 32:17; James 3:18).

Finally, this peace is an outgrowth of God's re-creation. In individuals, peace is the work of God's Spirit, peace is the effect of our being joined together in a harmoniously working whole. In Ephesians 2:15 this is said to be the work of Christ; it is also the work of the Spirit (v. 22). This peace is a fact, not a fancy; a present reality, not something to be hoped for. Where this peace is lacking, Christ and the Spirit are missing. The harmonious working together of the saints in the Body is guaranteed by the presence of the Spirit, and it must be the goal of every saint.

The Means to Cultivate This Fruit

The Bible is quite specific as to how this peace is to be

maintained so far as its human aspects are concerned. In the area of individual experience let us note the following:

1. *Conscious trust in the Lord:*

> You will keep him in perfect peace, whose mind is resting on you; because he trusts in you (Isa. 26:3).

"The emphasis upon steadfastness in this verse is striking, and possibly calls to mind the fact that the human heart by nature is not stable. It is a mind that wavers and changes with every shifting wind of doctrine, for it has no firm foundation upon which to rest. When it reposes upon the Lord, however, it abides firm and constant, preserved in His perfect peace, for it rests, not upon the changing sands of human opinion but upon God, the Rock eternal and unchangeable."[10]

2. *Belief of the Scriptures:*

> By this we shall know that we are of the Truth, and shall persuade our hearts before him: because if our heart condemns us, God is greater than our heart, and knows all things (1 John 3:19f).

True peace of mind is a consequence of the assurance of salvation. But how may such assurance be ours? John says, we may be assured when we see that God has given us a love for the brethren. So when our hearts and consciences accuse us we should remember that God is greater than our hearts, and He has forgiven us for all of which our hearts may accuse us. The promises of forgiveness are the source of peace to the needlessly troubled soul.

3. *Prayer and Thanksgiving*:

> Don't be anxious about anything; but in everything by prayer and supplication with thanksgiving let your requests be made known before God. And the peace of God which cannot be explained along ordinary lines will stand sentry over your hearts and minds in Christ Jesus (Phil. 4:6f).

If prayer begins because of some anxiety, it ends with peace. But the procedure involved in prayer is significant:

a. "Prayer," "supplication," and "requests" can probably be distinguished from each other only in that the first is general and refers to our state of mind in asking, while the last two refer to the specific requests themselves.

b. "Thanksgiving" must accompany true prayer because we never pray in a vacuum. The God to whom we are praying has blessed us in the past. We should not forget this. Nor should we forget that His wisdom may deny our specific petition, and for this we should be grateful. But in any case, the peace will come.

c. "Before God," as the Greek word implies. Prayer is not a message sent off to a far-distant God but is petition made in the presence of the omnipresent God. This is why prayer is communion. Prayer is not like a telegraph message sent impersonally through indifferent intermediaries, but it is conversation directly with the Lord of all the earth.

Examined in this light it is easy to see how, on the human level, prayer can bring peace. If we approach God in a humble state of mind, rejoicing in His past blessings, and lay specific petitions before Him, we induce thereby a certain state of well-being and calmness. But the apostle promises much more than this. There is an answer which is over and beyond all this — the peace which comes is, as we have seen, beyond any human device. It is an act of God, mysterious and ineffable as all acts of God must be, but it is real and definite beyond any cavil.

In the area of communal experience, let us note the following:

1. *By an awareness of the Body* (Eph. 4:3). Two Christian ministers were talking about a particularly tempestuous saint who had left their company. After the initial expressions of relief, one of them said, "But in the final analysis, we have not left each other. We are all still in the Body of Christ."

Christendom needs today a definitive study of the relation of the Church-as-invisible to the Church-as-visible. The doctrine is being perverted on every hand. But one thing is evident in all discussions — there is a Body of Christ on earth and it includes every person who has been received by Jesus

Christ; and the members of this Body are inseparably joined to each other with ties and interests and labors which are more significant than any other relationships one could imagine. If we grasp this point, we will then see that self-interest dictates working toward peace, because where one member of the body suffers, the whole body suffers. And when we remember that it is the Body *of Christ,* His majesty dictates that we work toward peace and harmony so that the Body will promote His glory among the nations.

2. *By observing God's order in the Church.*[11] Our churches have not been known for having unruly or disorderly worship services, and yet this must have been a problem among the Corinthians. In First Corinthians, chapters 11 and 14, Paul had to counsel for order and peace. In most churches this order is a responsibility of elders. They must determine from Scripture what order is best suited to their congregation, and they must see that this order is carried out whenever public worship is held. Churches today should not uncritically assume that the order to which they are accustomed is the only order permitted. Again, Christendom would benefit from a fresh study of the principles of public worship today.[12]

Our churches are better known for business meetings which have gone out of hand, and have sometimes become unruly. Paul speaks to this problem in First Thessalonians 5:12f. First, note that Paul describes the leaders as those "who labor among you, and are over you in the Lord and admonish you." Second, he describes the attitude to be taken toward the leaders: "know them," and "esteem them," "exceeding highly in love"! Finally, note Paul's final command which seems to be the result of the foregoing: "Be at peace among yourselves."

Elders are not to be so esteemed because of their Christian character, although they should not be elders unless they conform to the biblical standard; but "for their work's sake." This may mean, because they are engaged in God's work, or it may mean, because they are concerned for your souls.

In church disputes it is so easy to reject leaders because of defects in their character and then to substitute anarchy for order in the church. "God is not a God of confusion, but of peace."

In all we have said so far we have been concerned with peace in Christian circles. Something should be said about the responsibility of Christians for the peace of the world. Our Lord indicates that there will always be wars and disputes in the world, and that in particular that which is the fruit of the Spirit will never be found in the world. Some want to leave it at that and become disengaged from the world and watch it go its way to destruction. The Bible, I suggest, has something better for us.

Even the ancient Israelites, separated as they were from other nations, were told by Jeremiah that they had a personal stake in peace when they would be captives in Babylon: "And seek the peace of the city to which I have caused you to be carried away captive, and pray unto the Lord for it: for in its peace you shall have peace" (Jer. 29:7).

Even more emphatically Paul commands the Christians to pray for authorities "that we may lead a tranquil and quiet life in all godliness and gravity" (1 Tim. 2:2). There is a right way and a wrong way for churches to become involved in politics. As churches we should be prayer groups imploring the God of heaven to rule among the authorities. John Calvin puts it this way: "If any one ask, Ought we to pray for kings, from whom we obtain none of these advantages? I answer, the object of prayer is, that, guided by the Spirit of God, they may begin to impart to us those benefits of which they formerly deprived us. It is our duty, therefore, not only to pray for those who are already worthy, but we must pray to God that he may make bad men good. To this must be added that, if we are deprived of those benefits the communication of which Paul assigns to magistrates, that is through our own fault. It is the wrath of God that renders magistrates useless to us, in the same manner that it renders the earth barren; and, therefore we ought to pray for the removal of those chastisements which have been brought upon us by our sins."[13]

Moreover when war comes, it is incumbent on the individual Christian to decide whether he may take up arms, "upon just and necessary occasion."[14] Christian conscience, much more than patriotism, should dictate the conduct of young men who are called upon to wage war. And the Christian community should protect the consciences of those who, for good reasons of conscience, cannot take up arms in any given occasion.

Questions for Chapter 7

1. How can we have peace with someone who doesn't want it?
2. Does the Bible teach a spirit of "peace at any price" among the saints?
3. Has God given us a criterion for determining whether a war is a righteous one?
4. Is it possible for us to have God's peace and still have differences of opinion?
5. Why is "peace" frequently a synonym for "salvation"?
6. How is peace related to the other fruit?

Notes

[1] The Hebrew word for "peace."

[2] *Biblical Commentary on the Proverbs of Solomon,* Vol. I, p. 146.

[3] *Ibid.*, pp. 148f.

[4] Arndt and Gingrich, *A Greek-English Lexicon of the New Testament,* p. 868.

[5] Theodore Laetsch, *Bible Commentary*, p. 84.

[6] Philippians 4:6f.

[7] Lightfoot, *Saint Paul's Epistle to the Philippians* (Zondervan Publishing House), p. 161.

[8] KJV has "preparation."

[9] Lightfoot, *St. Paul's Epistles to the Colossians and to Philemon* (Zondervan Publishing House), p. 223.

[10] E. J. Young, *The Book of Isaiah,* Vol. II, p. 208.

[11] Cf. especially 1 Cor. 14:26-40; 1 Thess. 5:12f.

[12] Cf. Appendix.

[13] *Commentaries on the First Epistle to Timothy*, p. 52.

[14] *Westminster Confession of Faith*, Chap. XXIII, Sec. II.

Chapter 8

Patience

IF THE GALATIANS were losing their joy and peace, the weed of impatience would soon be forcing its ugly way into the garden of their hearts. We may modify Burton's definition of "patience" a bit and say, *Patience is steadfastness in obedience to God despite pressure to deny Him.*[1] Where love and joy and peace are lacking, it is difficult to resist invitations to explode in impatience.

The world is full of pressures; they are here because of sin; they are here because of the curse which God has placed on the world and its activities. God's people are not immune to them: "In the world you will have tribulation." To His Father Jesus said, "I do not pray that you should take them out of the world, but that you should keep them from the evil one." This is all the greater reason then for seeking God's grace which will see us through times of difficulty and incitements to deny Him.

THE WEED TO BE ROOTED OUT

The impatient man has some reason to be upset. He sees injustice, or harm being inflicted, or perhaps things are not going according to some preconceived plan. The impatient man becomes angry and takes matters into his own hands. He is short-tempered and quick to anger. Let us note a few instances of this:

1. *Impatience With God's Timetable*

Why is it that tires go flat when we are in a hurry to keep an appointment? Or, why does the vacuum cleaner stop working the day when company is coming? But more important, why are we so unhappy and frustrated when these things occur?

In essence our resentment is against the timetable which the sovereign God has assigned to us, a schedule based on a plan of which we are usually ignorant. It is this ignorance which brings about our frustration, the seeming senselessness of delay, loss, or failure. But this is the reason why impatience is such a noxious weed — it leaves God out of our thinking. It is another case of practical atheism.

One may wonder why I emphasize this practical atheism. Is this really so bad after all, or aren't there worse sins? Practical atheism is a snub directed at God. It ignores Him and He resents a snub just as we do when others "look through" us in contempt. Our God is an intensely emotional being, "a jealous God" He calls Himself, and so He abhors practical atheism.

King Saul ignored God's timetable (1 Sam. 13:8ff), and for this he lost the opportunity of having his sons follow him on the throne of Israel. Kirkpatrick[2] comments: "Saul's sin seems excusable and scarcely deserving of so heavy a punishment. But it involved the whole principle of the subordination of the theocratic king to the Will of Jehovah as expressed by His prophets. On the one hand it showed a distrust of God, as though God after choosing him for this work could forsake him in the hour of need: on the other hand it showed a spirit of self-assertion, as though he could make war by himself without the assistance and counsel of God communicated through His prophet. Such a character was unfit for the office of king."

2. *Impatience Under Trial*

Some of the recipients of James' letter were evidently people who were especially put upon. They seem to have been poor workers who were mistreated by rich employers, and the heinousness of the employers' sin was so great that they brought upon themselves one of the most stinging denunciations in all of the Holy Scriptures (James 5:1-6). Under these circumstances it would have been natural to be impatient. After all, we live only once, and if in that life we are denied basic freedoms, we feel a certain sense of justification in being impatient.

Probably nothing seemed more natural to Peter than to strike out at the soldier who was in the act of arresting Jesus. Peter's impatience made him do a silly thing, and as it turned out, a wicked thing. We should not try to cast Peter's action into a heroic mold; it was not the valor of fighting against great odds, it was disobedience against the command of God. Peter had to understand, as James' readers had to understand, that Jesus did not come into the world to condemn it, but to save men, and often God's means of saving men puts His own people into difficult places. To act rashly and impatiently under such circumstances might mean the loss of an opportunity for testimony.

The time for judgment will come, and at that time the Righteous One will mete out a condemnation which fits the crime. Under pressure we may be too lenient, or too harsh. This is why patience befits the Christian who believes in a wise God. To be impatient, to take matters into our own hands, either denies God's prerogative to judge, or else raises doubts as to His capacity to do so. This is why impatience is a weed.

3. *Impatience With Another's Weaknesses*

If we return to the James 5 passage, we will note that the apostle is concerned not only with the reaction of the saints to the persecution which was coming to them from without; he warned also against their murmuring against one another within the Christian community itself (v. 9), and he urges patience among the saints.

This weed grows rampant in the world. Hardly a day passes but one hears sneering remarks about the stupidity, the awkwardness, the ineptitude of others; and many such remarks are made regarding things and actions for which the person accused is not responsible. What is objected to then is that God has made them that way! Once again the impatience is directed against God.

But the weed has not been cleared from the Church. One of the most divisive spirits within the Christian community is impatience with another's weakness and sins. It is painful to hear responsible Christians speaking disdainfully of "young Christians" and "babes in Christ" with a contempt which matches that of the world. The fact of the matter is that we may not require adult conduct of children. When we see this in the physical world, we laugh. But when new converts are immediately expected, and sometimes required, to adopt the mores set for them by older Christians, then we have a noxious weed indeed.

The Artificial Fruit to Be Detected

Sometimes we are struck by the seeming ability of people to endure all kinds of adversities. Endurance may be a gift of God, or it may be a counterfeit. Some people are just too lazy to react; others may be so proud that they will not dignify their attackers with a response. Some of us are by nature more insensitive to criticism than others and hence have an appearance of long-suffering. Some by ordinary human calculation will endure a temporary hardship to gain a long-range advantage.

What we must emphasize here is the source of the long-suffering and the motive for it. It is what makes people endure that counts. Christianity is not a mere ethic. Many make a great mistake right here when they confuse the Gospel with the teachings of, say, Plato or the Stoics. Superficially there may be likeness. But Paul is calling true patience[3] a fruit of the Spirit, unattainable by any merely human contrivance.

Such patience must somehow, sooner or later, appear to be divine in source and motivation. This is possibly one of the reasons for persecutions in the history of the Church. Perhaps only in the fires of such persecutions can real patience be seen; but perhaps not. A renewed emphasis on the fruit of the Spirit may bring again a type of spiritual power which will exceed the best of the world's ethics, not only in the great moments of persecution, but also in the little details of daily living when we are called upon to show a steadfastness in obedience to God despite pressure to deny Him.

The Fruit to Be Cultivated

The seed which the Spirit has planted is a continued awareness of the presence of God.

We have had occasion to remark (p. 42) on the interrelatedness of the fruit of the Spirit, and nowhere is this more evident than in patience. It does not stand alone; it supports and is supported by other Christian virtues. So frequently is it mentioned along with these other characteristics that one may say that without "kindness," "love," "knowledge," "faith," and "hope," one cannot be patient.[4]

We begin our study of patience with Jesus' parable in Matthew 18:21. Peter wanted to put a limit on human patience: "How often shall my brother sin against me, and I forgive him?" To answer, Jesus tells the story of the steward whose master responded without limit to the steward's request for patience (v. 26). But that same steward showed no patience at all to a fellow-servant even though he used the very same words as he asked for patience on the steward's part (v. 29). The upshot of the parable — "And his lord was angry, and delivered him to the tormentors, till he should pay all that was due. So shall also my heavenly Father do to you, if you forgive not every one his brother from your hearts."

Now this passage should teach us that God's patience is so powerful a force that it cannot but be reflected in those who have asked for and received His patience. "How often shall my brother sin against me, and I forgive him?" receives its answer in the words, "Should you not also have had mercy on your fellow-servant, even as I had mercy on you?" (v. 33).

God's long-suffering must be understood against the background of wrath and a day of reckoning. Long-suffering does not mean in itself that the basis for anger has been removed (that idea is expressed by "grace" and "justification"); it stresses the fact that a reckoning has been made and that wrath is deserved, but it is being withheld. We see this especially in the Old Testament where God is described as "long of wrath" as the Hebrew might be translated literally, that is, "slow to anger" (Ex. 34:6).

But patience is also expressed in endurance, perseverance, and especially steadfastness. Paul reminds Timothy of his own long-suffering in various places, but this could not be construed as softness or passivity (2 Tim. 3:10). Moreover Timothy was to follow Paul's example (4:2) and "reprove, rebuke, exhort with all long-suffering and doctrine." Paul did not compromise his doctrine by patience. Patience was the atmosphere in which he stood fast and preached the doctrines of grace.

We cannot have patience unless we have knowledge, faith, and hope as well. A man can be patient if he understands what is going on in a given situation. Ignorance breeds impatience. So does inexperience. This is why children are naturally impatient. But trouble produces patience (Rom. 5:3), for after we have come through some difficulty we can face it again, or one like it, without impatience because we know what is happening.

Similarly, faith is an ingredient of patience. Christian patience is based on the belief that a sovereign God is at work in men's affairs, and it springs from the expectancy that a believer will not be mocked or forgotten by the God to whose keeping he has committed his soul. Just as the weed of impatience grows in an atmosphere which leaves God out of our thinking, so the fruit of the Spirit which is patience grows where there is a continual awareness of God.

Long-suffering must also be oriented to the Christian's eschatology. Note the number of times the second coming of Christ is introduced in a context when patience is under discussion.[5]

We return to James 5, where the apostle makes our understanding of patience more concrete by giving us three examples of it:

1. *The Patience of a Farmer* (v. 7)

Every farmer knows that under ordinary conditions the time for harvest cannot be hastened. There are laws of maturation in the physical world, and man must submit to them. In a real sense this is steadfastness in obedience to God and is therefore a good example for activities in the spiritual world. There, too, laws obtain and while they may not be the same sorts of laws, we must be patient until their time for fulfillment.

One outstanding example of such long-suffering is the refusal of David to take Saul's life, even though he had many provocations and pressures to do so. But David understood that God's law had a date on it. Once again, we must call attention to the difference between laziness and true patience. One might use this principle as an excuse for doing nothing; what this principle calls for is not inactivity but it calls for refusing to act in a certain way and for a certain period of time.

But our principle is broader than calling for an obedience to known laws; it calls for trust in God when events occur which are seemingly senseless or wasteful; that is, when we have no reason to be patient, but perhaps every reason to be impatient. This brings us to

2. *The Patience of a Martyr* (v. 10)

A martyr suffers not because of evil-doing but because of good behavior (1 Peter 3:17), and a martyr's reward is given to the man who "bears up under sorrows when suffering unjustly. For what credit is there if, when you sin and are harshly treated, you endure it with patience? But if when you do what is right and suffer for it you patiently endure it, this finds favor with God" (1 Peter 2:19, 20).

The writer to the Hebrews writes that Old Testament martyrs were "men of whom the world was not worthy" (11:38). Jesus certainly did nót predict a soft life for His disciples (John 16:2ff), and He warned against being too well-accepted by society — that was a characteristic of false prophets in the Old Testament!

All this means that a martyr's patience, being a fruit of the Spirit and not a characteristic of an unbeliever, should be a subject of special cultivation by the Christian. To suffer for well-doing, to suffer without rational explanation; to expect good only from the hand of God and even that perhaps not in this world — this is the character God seeks among men.

3. *The Patience of Job* (v. 11)

But what about it when even God seems to deal unfairly with us? This was Job's complaint, and for a long time God did nothing to relieve Job's ignorance. Job seems to have had temporary lapses of patience, but each lapse seems to have driven him to some new insight of faith. What Job did not know about his special and unique circumstances, he received manifold compensation for in his glimpses of the resurrection. James reminds us that "the outcome of the Lord's dealings" was "that the Lord is full of compassion and is merciful."

God does not tell us all we should like to know about our circumstances. There are many "secret things" which belong to the Lord. God does not place much store on mere knowledge, but He does expect great patience on the part of His saints who frequently must endure when God, man, and circumstances seem to be against them. "Behold we count them blessed who endure" (James 5:11).

The Means to Cultivate This Fruit

What will enable us to be steadfast in our obedience to God? Trouble, says Paul in Romans 5:3. But doesn't trouble make us impatient? Trouble alone will every time, but Paul connects the trouble which produces patience with the faith that justifies and which gives access into the grace by which we stand. Faith in God makes for continued awareness of the presence of God.

In the epistle to the Romans Paul is refreshingly naive — He really believes that the Christian will respond to trouble as a Christian should! Trouble, says Paul, makes a Christian patient because the next time trouble comes the Christian will reflect that it wasn't all that bad, that help did come, and that when it passed he felt the better for it.

1. *It wasn't all that bad*. Every trial is really bearable, for it has happened before and will happen again to others. That's what Paul means by "common to man" in 1 Corinthians 10:13. In fact, everything which happens to a Christian, God here promises, is only run of the mine. The only truly unique trouble happened to Jesus, and we are not called upon to bear that.

2. *Help did come*. Every trial has a way out, provided by the faithfulness of God. Paul was quite alone when he wrote to Timothy the second time. "At my first defense no one took my part, but all forsook me. . . . But the Lord stood by me . . . and I was delivered out of the mouth of the lion" (2 Tim. 4:16f).

God's faithfulness is particularly evident when we are alone, for then it does not have to vie in our minds with human devices. And it was in his loneliness that Paul shows his great patience: "The Lord will deliver me from every evil work." It never occurred to Paul that God would ever leave him, and so he could with patience await the next ordeal.

3. *He felt the better for it*. Patience has her perfect work; we are glad for the trouble after we have endured it. This has been one of the themes of hymnody through the years:

> With mercy and with judgment my web of time He wove,
> And aye the dews of sorrow were lustered by His love.
> I'll bless the hand that guided, I'll bless the heart that planned,
> When throned where glory dwelleth in Immanuel's land.

As the shadows fall on western civilization, the saints had

better major in patience. It may be all that will be left to us. Twice in Revelation (13:10 and 14:12), John calls God's people to patience. In both instances, as the earth reels under the blows of destruction, some self-inflicted, some God-inflicted, the saints are counseled to believe that God is on the throne, that in His good time righteousness will prevail; and in the meantime, amid the trouble — "here is the patience and faith of the saints."

Questions for Chapter 8

1. "Practical atheism" may be related to the other fruit as well as to patience. Show how we cannot have the fruit unless we have true faith.
2. How can we be patient with new converts, and at the same time urge them on in holiness?
3. The Greek New Testament uses two words for patience: one has the idea of "bearing up under"; the other, "long endurance." Show that examples of patience in the Bible really include both ideas.
4. Does patience ever lead to apathy? If you think so, tell how inactivity may be avoided.
5. How is patience related to the other fruit?

Notes

[1] E. D. Burton, *A Critical and Exegetical Commentary on the Epistle to the Galatians*, p. 315.

[2] Kirkpatrick, *Cambridge Bible*, 1 Samuel, p. 126.

[3] There are two words for "patience" in the New Testament. For all practical purposes they are synonyms and will be so treated in the discussion which follows.

[4] Cf. the following lists: Rom. 2:4: goodness and forbearance and long-suffering; 1 Cor. 13:4f: love suffers long, is kind, . . . rejoices with the truth, . . . hopes all things; 2 Cor. 6:6: in pureness, in knowledge, in long-suffering, in kindness, in the Holy Spirit, in love unfeigned; Col. 3:12: a heart of compassion, kindness, lowliness, meekness, long-suffering.

[5] Cf. Luke 21:19ff; Rom. 8:25; 1 Thess. 1:3; 2 Thess. 3:5; Heb. 10:36; James 5:7.

Chapter 9

Kindness

WE COME NOW to two words whose meanings are so similar that in other parts of the Scriptures, and in the Greek Old Testament, they are used as synonyms. Neither word occurs very frequently. In the King James Version the words are translated as "gentleness" and "goodness." With some hesitation we are following the example of more modern versions which render them as "kindness" and "goodness." As will be seen we are not rejecting "gentleness" as a fruit, for many of its facets will appear under "meekness."

The question may well arise, why not treat these words as synonyms, and combine the discussions of them into one chapter? After all, Paul has a habit of enforcing a point by heaping up synonyms and near-synonyms.

In this listing, on the other hand, where all the other words have a meaning of their own, it seems odd that Paul would use these two with exactly the same meaning. Hence, the separate treatment.

It must be kept in mind, however, that we are dealing with

the "fruit," not the "fruits" of the Spirit. Christian character is of one piece, and inevitably one trait will blend into another under close examination.

The Judaizers' teaching was making the Galatians selfish. Since they had to please God by their own works, their personal concerns soon took precedence over any claim someone else had on their time. Selfishness was leading to all sorts of evil thinking and evil acting. How could the Galatians' eyes be opened to their peril?

Perhaps if they could see the weeds for what they are, and the fruit for what it is — the very seeing of them might help. So Paul writes in Galatians 5:19ff: " . . . enmities, strife, jealousies, wraths, factions, divisions, parties, envyings, . . . kindness . . . "

The Weed to Be Rooted Out

Selfishness is a daughter of pride. For a man to be selfish, he has to feel that he has the right to be selfish; and this right is easily conferred on him by pride. He has every reason to seek his own pleasure and well-being because he is convinced that he has achieved a place of merit and honor unique among men. Pride justifies selfishness, and pride is a noxious weed, but it has several manifestations. Let us look at some concrete instances of them.

1. *The Trouble-making of Diotrephes* (3 John 9-10)

As we noted elsewhere (p. 77ff), Diotrephes was a pretty imperious fellow because he wanted to be first. His selfishness led him to reject John's words. But soon he went beyond this and began "unjustly accusing us with wicked words," and rejected the brethren. A man simply cannot feed his ego and also look for the needs of other people. Diotrephes was not a kind man. He was a bully, a liar, and a rebel against God's order in the church. He was no good to anyone, not even himself.

2. *The Rebellion of Moses' Lieutenants* (Numbers 12:1-3; 16:1ff)

Twice during the wilderness wanderings men resented Moses' authority and led an abortive rebellion. Each time the motive of their rebellion was self-seeking, and the root of the self-seeking was pride.

At Kibroth-hattaavah, the people had seen a demonstration of Moses' authority and human dignity. He had gathered seventy elders and God appeared to them, taking a visible form of the Spirit which was upon Moses and sharing Him with the seventy. Moses' burden was not only lightened, but the people could see in a fresh way how he was truly their mediator and leader.

But, said Miriam[1] and Aaron to each other, we have our place too. Moses isn't the only one who has the Spirit and the right to honors from the people. Had not Miriam been a prophetess (Ex. 15:20)? Did not Aaron carry the Urim and Thummim which gave guidance to the people? "They pride themselves on their gift of prophecy, which ought rather to have schooled them to humility. But such is the natural depravity of men, not only to abuse the gifts of God unto contempt of their brethren, but so to magnify them by their ungodly and sacrilegious boasting, as to obscure the glory of their Author."[2]

Thus spurred on by pride and selfishness, they rebuked their brother openly at a time when he needed all the encouragement he could get. For this unkind act Miriam suffered grievously: first, the humiliation before all the people when she turned leprous; and then the banishment for seven days until her time of uncleanness because of the leprosy was over.

A few chapters later (Num. 16:1ff), another rebellion springs from selfishness and pride. Korah led a movement of princes of the congregation, protesting that Moses and Aaron took too much on themselves. After all, had not God said that the whole congregation was holy?[3] What was so special about those two?

> The rebels appeal to the calling of all Israel to be the holy nation of Jehovah, and infer from this the equal right of all to

hold the priesthood, leaving entirely out of sight, as blind selfishness is accustomed to do, the transition of the universal priesthood into the special mediatorial office and priesthood of Moses and Aaron, which had their foundation in fact (Baumgarten); or altogether overlooking the fact that God Himself had chosen Moses and Aaron, and appointed them as mediators between Himself and the congregation, to educate the sinful nation, and train it to the fulfillment of its proper vocation. The rebels, on the contrary, thought that they were holy already, because God had called them to be a holy nation, and in their carnal self-righteousness forgot the condition attached to their calling, "If you will obey my voice indeed, and keep my covenant."[4]

3. *The Sulking of Jonah* (Jonah 4:1ff)

Jonah was a bright, intelligent man; and he knew something about Israel's God. So Jonah knew that although God was angry at Nineveh, if Nineveh repented then God would not punish them according to Jonah's message. All this Jonah seems to have thought, or perhaps even said to God, even before he went to Nineveh (cf. 4:2). Sure that this was the case, Jonah fled to Tarshish. But God intervened, Jonah repented and obeyed the second command to announce the destruction of the great city.

The people, as we know, reacted with great outward demonstrations of repentance, and "God saw their works, that they turned from their evil way; and God repented of the evil which he said he would do to them; and he didn't do it."

Jonah was irked, angry at God. Why? Some suggest that he was humiliated because his prophecy was not fulfilled — he had been made a fool of in the sight of the heathen. But the text seems to indicate that Jonah was proud of his nationality, and selfish for its supremacy among the nations.[5] His pride and selfishness led to an attitude of unkindness which the Lord rebuked: "Should not I have regard for Nineveh, that great city, in which there are more than 120,000 who cannot discern between their right hand and their left hand; and also much cattle?"

God had become the God of Israel only that through them

He might also be the God of all the families of the earth. Jonah knew this, and he knew that God was compassionate, but his nationalistic feelings got the better of his correct doctrine, and he became rebellious against God and unkind toward the Ninevites.

Pride and selfishness and unkindness do not mix with the life which God calls His people to live. But, as the above examples show, they do mix quite readily with a false view of Christianity. The Pharisees were very religious, but they placed intolerable burdens on the people who were following their teachings (cf. Matt. 23:4). The Judaizers were doing the same thing to the Galatians. This is one reason why our relations with other people are an indicator of our own spiritual health. Where there is unkindness, there is something wrong inside.

In the four instances we have examined, Diotrephes' willfulness, Miriam and Aaron's rebellion, Korah's insurrection, and Jonah's sulking — it is important to note that unkindness to others was produced by selfishness and pride, and these are closely linked to disobedience and rebellion toward God. Our attitudes toward our fellowmen are a result of, and perhaps an indication of, our relation to God. Unkindness then is a noxious weed because it breaks both of the great commandments at once.

Would the Galatians want to be like Miriam or Jonah or Diotrephes, and to receive their punishment? Or did God have something better for them?

The Artificial Fruit to Be Detected

Not all men are unkind. All men are not unkind all the time, for a certain sort of kindness has real value. It can be used to manipulate people so that the one who shows kindness can gain his ends.

The Bible gives us a few gross examples of this artificial fruit: Jacob showed kindness to Esau (Gen. 25:27), and deprived him of his birthright; Jael treated Sisera to a bottle of milk and a few moments of rest (Judg. 4:18ff), and then took his life as he slept; Delilah spoke words of love to Samson (Judg. 16:4ff), and robbed him of his power as a judge in Israel.

But there are more subtle ways to show kindness in order to gain one's ends. The judges in Israel were forbidden to receive gifts from the people; this might pervert their sense of justice because it turned their eyes from issues to the people involved. Similarly, saints manipulate one another by bestowing honors, gifts, and rewards.

Satan was persuaded that God's kindness to Job was like that, that God had so blessed Job that he would never depart from Him — it would not be economically worthwhile! But God's kindness is not bestowed for base ends, and Job suffered as he did to demonstrate that God was not manipulating him, but redeeming him.

Then Satan tried to offer the artificial fruit to Jesus Christ. He showed Him all kingdoms of the world in a moment of time and said, "I will give all this authority, and all their glory to you, . . . if you will worship me" (Luke 4:5ff). But the Son of God was not to be manipulated.

Nor should we manipulate each other. There is a method for gaining our ends in this world. We call it prayer. It is "an offering up of our desires to God, for things, agreeable to his will, in the name of Christ, with confession of our sins, and thankful acknowledgment of his mercies."[6] When we learn to pray, we will not be so prone to cultivate the artificial fruit of manipulation.

The Fruit to Be Cultivated

In his description of our redemption in Ephesians 2:4ff, Paul uses a number of words to describe God's love toward us: "rich in mercy," "great love," "grace," "kindness." Again in Titus 3:4, he brings together "kindness" and "love toward men." Kindness is an attribute of God, and this attribute is re-created in men at the moment of their new birth.

As we noted at the beginning of this chapter "kindness" is

not used frequently in the New Testament, but examples of kindness abound. Before New Testament times, the Greeks spoke of things as "useful," "serviceable," "effective"; and of people as "outgoing," "useful," and "benevolent."[7] In doing so they used the root from which our word "kindness" is taken. In many New Testament passages we see examples of such "usefulness" but perhaps no more clearly than in the actions of the "good Samaritan" (Luke 10:25-37).

A lawyer asked Jesus how he might attain eternal life. Jesus asked him, "What does the Bible say?" The lawyer replied, but wished to justify his conduct — he had not treated all people equally — and so inquired, "Who is my neighbor?" It was fashionable in his day to interpret the Old Testament to mean that love for all men equally was not required. In particular, love need not be shown to Samaritans, for they were enemies, of a mixed racial stock and therefore inferior, and perverters of the Old Testament religion, for they received only the five books of Moses (and even them in a corrupted form).

In the parable Jesus spoke of a man in dire need — he had been robbed, beaten, left half-dead. Who would show him kindness? Not a priest, not a levite. These were the upper classes among the Jews, the examples of virtue which lower classes would follow. They were neither kind nor merciful. But the Samaritan was! Jesus was exposing the self-righteous pride of many of the Jews of His day. Their pride led to unkindness. The Samaritan had nothing to be proud of. He was moved with compassion, bound up the man's wounds after having treated them with oil and wine, carried him to an inn for recovery, and paid his expenses while recuperating.

The real question was not, who is my neighbor? as though I could make a list of those who are and those who are not. Jesus raised and answered the real question, to whom should I act as a neighbor? His answer, I should be a neighbor to whoever needs me.[8] Kindness is availability, usefulness, benevolence, outgoingness.

These are the meanings we should read into "selflessness" (in contrast to "selfishness" mentioned on p. 98ff). In kindness, we should give ourselves to others. Recall that this was Paul's motive for visiting Rome: "that I may impart some spiritual gift to you, that you may be established" (Rom. 1:11).

This is why Paul uses "kindness" to describe God. See how kind He has been to us. He has given us all we need for this life, and for the life to come.

THE MEANS TO CULTIVATE THIS FRUIT

Perhaps Jesus used the Samaritan as an example of neighborliness for more reasons than one. It was certainly to show that Samaritans could receive the grace to be kind, as well as the Jews. But perhaps Jesus wanted the lawyer to see that one had to become like a Samaritan — socially outcast, undone, without pride or status — before he could learn to be kind. Just as pride produces unkindness, so humility produces kindness.

But, you will say, do other people really need *me*? And need me desperately?

Listen to a lonely man: "At my first defense no one supported me, but all deserted me; may it not be counted against them" (2 Tim. 4:16). Think how much good one insignificant saint might have done to Paul!

Listen to the same apostle, some years earlier: "The eye cannot say to the hand, 'I have no need of you'; or again the head to the feet, 'I have no need of you.' " Paul wants us to see that when we withdraw from others (withhold our help from them on the false-modesty principle that we are no good), we do greater harm to the Body of Christ than a disabled hand or foot does to your physical body. The tragedy today is that Christ's Body is in a wheelchair because so many parts of it are "going it alone."

Part of our difficulty is a doctrinal inbalance. We are all crushed by the doctrine of sin and its implications: we feel guilty (and we should!), helpless (because we are!), worthless (and we sing, "Two wonders I confess, The wonders of redeeming love, And my own worthlessness").

But there is another doctrine which may not be ignored: we have been raised from the ashes of penitence to a dignity beyond our appreciation. Ephesians 1:18 contains an amazing statement: "the glorious riches of his inheritance in the saints." An inheritance cannot be cheap or useless. An inheritance is valuable. The saints are valuable in Christ's sight: those worthless, useless, helpless sinners are now an inheritance which Christ cherishes and values. As Dr. J. Oliver Buswell Jr. once paraphrased this verse: "He has made you worth-while."

What the newborn Christian sees then, is that he is a part of a community all of whose members need him, his prayers, his time, his money, his talents. These he cannot deny to fellow-believers.

But he sees still another outlet for his kindness. There is the community of the world in which he remains as salt to preserve it, as light to give it hope, as priest to bring members of it to God.

The Christian cannot be a loner. The greater his love for God, the greater will be his involvement for kindness among others.

This is why Jesus closed His conversation with the lawyer with these words: "Go, and continue doing likewise" (Luke 10:37). The fact that a Samaritan showed mercy on a Jew (for it is probable that we are intended to infer that the injured man was a Jew) teaches us that we must show kindness to men of every race and creed. The fact that Jesus used the present tense in His application of the parable teaches us that this is a life-long task.

Unfortunately evangelicals so stress the individual character of salvation that there is little thought of its corporate character. It is just this overemphasis on the individual that makes us so unkind to each other, and unkind to our fellowmen. We are individuals, but we are also members of communities — families, churches, neighborhoods, office forces, labor unions — and in them we are desperately needed by our fellows.

Questions for Chapter 9

1. If we are called to kindness, should we ever show anger, indignation or shock at an instance of evil?
2. Is there any limit to kindness? Suppose someone makes unreasonable demands on me and my time?
3. What does it mean to have "a broken and contrite heart"? Describe someone in that state. What outward characteristics would he have?
4. Why is genuine kindness so lacking in the world today? Among Christians today? What can we do to restore it?
5. How is kindness related to the other fruit?

Notes

[1] It seems clear that Miriam was the leader in this, Aaron the follower. Not only is she mentioned first, but the verb form in v. 1 is feminine.

[2] Calvin, *Commentaries on the Four Last Books of Moses*, Vol. IV, p. 43f.

[3] Exodus 19:5, 6.

[4] Delitzsch, *Biblical Commentary on the Old Testament: The Pentateuch*, Vol. III, p. 106f.

[5] Doubtless Jonah foresaw the rise of Assyria, at his time a relatively weak kingdom, and understood what it might do to Israel. His place, however, was to obey God and to leave the consequences to Him.

[6] *The Shorter Catechism* #98

[7] Liddell and Scott, *A Greek-English Lexicon*, p. 2007.

[8] Arndt in his *Bible Commentary: St. Luke*, p. 291, puts it well: " 'Neighbor' is used not in the sense of 'a person who needs my help,' but 'a person who is able to, and who does, furnish the help required.' We use the adjective 'neighborly' in a corresponding significance."

Chapter 10

Goodness

IF, AS MANY MODERN scholars believe, the Galatian churches were founded during Paul's first missionary journey, then the Galatians had a concrete, living example of the "goodness" which is the fruit of the Spirit. Paul's fellow traveler was Barnabas. Just a little while before, Barnabas had brought blessing to the church in Antioch. As he reports the visit, Luke adds the words, "for he was a good man, full of the Holy Spirit and of faith" (Acts 11:24).

The Galatians therefore had seen an example of the fruit of the Spirit which is "goodness." But what was the weed which contrasted with goodness? A frequent contrast in the Scriptures is "evil," "bad." But what do we mean by these words?

THE WEED TO BE ROOTED OUT

Occasionally in the Scriptures an individual may be chosen by God to represent and illustrate an important teaching. Thus Abraham's life is characterized by faith; Isaac's by submission; Jacob's by grace. Sometimes a nation may represent, symbolically and typically, a particular facet of doctrine. Amalek appears on the pages of Scripture as the epitome of evil, and a study of his history may shed light on what "evil" really is.

Amalek comes into prominence in Exodus 17:8ff and Deuteronomy 25:17ff. He attacked Israel at Rephidim; he struck from the rear where the injured and tired had been sent; his attack was crucial because it came at a time when God's people were close to their destination, Sinai, where the covenant would be initiated. Of particular interest to us is the place of prayer in the defeat of Amalek. It was not an ordinary victory won by the might of arms. Nor was God present with His people in the usual sense, directing the strategy and working fear in the hearts of the enemy. Moses prayed on a mountaintop and when his hands were lifted up, Israel prevailed; when he grew tired, Amalek prevailed. The lesson is plain: Amalek was not an ordinary enemy, to be defeated by ordinary means; Amalek was spiritual evil and could be defeated only when spiritual weapons were brought into action.

God pronounced perpetual enmity between Himself and Amalek. The latter was to be utterly destroyed (Ex. 17:14). There was to be no possibility of redemption — Amalek was the epitome of evil.

Here we see "evil" and God's attitude toward it. It is rebellion, that which opposes God and endeavors to thwart His purposes; it destroys and harms what is good. But there are other examples of evil in the Bible.

Evil came into fuller expression in the person of Antiochus Epiphanes, that great persecutor of the Jewish people during the Maccabean period. Of him Daniel writes, he "shall do according to his will; and he shall exalt himself, and magnify himself against every god, and shall speak marvelous things against the God of gods" (11:36). The books of the Maccabees tell of his persecutions of the Jews: he robbed the temple, slew many thousands, prohibited temple worship, and tried to substitute a pagan service. For this he was called the "abomination of desolation." "In connection with this act of profanation great cruelties were practiced. Women who had circumcised their children were put to death, the infants being hanged about their necks. Those who had copies of the law in their possession were put to death by decree of the king, and the books themselves were torn and burned."[1]

A more subtle, less dramatic, but nonetheless heinous manifestation of evil was Judas Iscariot. He was "the son of perdition," sent to thwart the progress of the Gospel; and he did so, Satan having entered into him (John 13:27). The Bible's descriptions of Satan and his deed are reserved; Judas wrote his own epitaph — "Judas Iscariot who also betrayed him."

The fullest expression of evil in human history will be the "man of sin," whom Paul describes as "the lawless one . . . whose coming is according to the working of Satan with all power and signs and lying wonders, and with all deceit of unrighteousness" (2 Thess. 2:8ff).

It should be apparent from this review that "evil" is essentially a religious term. At the root it expresses antagonism and disobedience toward God. It is that force which destroys, ruins, harms, and renders ugly. It is the weed pre-eminent. It is worthless, cancerous, and degrading. But it is also an ethical term. "Wicked works result from a primal decision which is brought about by Satan as redemption and salvation are brought about by God."[2] Seen in this light "evil" is the root of all "evils."

As it works its way into the light of day evil takes on many forms. It can make a Jacob work deliberately to harm others. Before he met God, Jacob had nothing to commend him. He schemed, stole, lied, and cheated. One cannot read the Genesis account without "feeling sorry" for Esau, for his brother was evil. He was a rebel, and wholeheartedly disobedient.

Evil can also make a Christian impute evil motives to others (so I interpret 1 Cor. 13:5) and rejoice in another's misfortune (v. 6; cf. also Prov. 17:5). These twin weeds, so alien to Christian love, are related to the party-spirit which Paul mentions among the works of the flesh. They ruin the reputations of others, and they are a root of bitterness within, eating away at one's virtue until only ruin is left.

Paul's enemies were guilty of the former. In Thessalonica they spread around rumors of "uncleanness," "flattery," "covetousness," "seeking glory" (cf. 1 Thess. 2:3ff), thus trying to undermine Paul and his ministry.

Christ's enemies were guilty of the latter. "He saved others, but he can't save himself," they taunted. Somehow the spectacle of a human being writhing in pain gave them pleasure. Similarly the spectacle of another's failure, or loss, or pain can give us pleasure, especially if he isn't on our side. This weed, in all its ugliness, grows wherever rebellion against God appears.

And it was appearing in Galatia, all because the purity of the gospel message was being marred by the Judaizers. The antidote to evil *is* the Gospel; evil cannot be overcome except by the power of the Gospel. At the beginning of the letter Paul had reminded his readers that Jesus "gave himself for our sins, that he might deliver us out of this present evil world" (1:4). But to depart from Jesus is to place one's self under the control of evil.

The Artificial Fruit to Be Detected

Evil doesn't like to appear evil, so it has developed a goodly face. We call it "hypocrisy"; David Smith[3] called it "play-acting." It gives the appearance of goodness, with the motive of evil.

All men are hypocrites. Differences between men are due to the extent to which they are able to control their hypocrisies. But God is not fooled, and the artificial fruit of hypocrisy He despises more than the weed of evil.

We see this in one of the most disturbing verses of the Bible — Jeremiah 3:11, "The backslider, Israel, has shown herself to be more righteous than the faithless Judah." This verse is disturbing when we consider who Israel and Judah were. Israel was the northern kingdom, its capital, Samaria. For political reasons the people did not cross the border to worship at the divinely designated place, Jerusalem. Moreover the kings of Israël were not of Judah, the tribe appointed by God to rule His people. So Israel had neither a lawful form of worship, accredited priests, nor kings with authority to rule. Besides all this, Israel's apostasy from God was unrelieved by revivals during the 210 years of its existence, despite the powerful ministry of Amos, Elijah, Elisha, and others.

Israel was the modernist wing of the people of God!

Now compare Judah with Israel: she had the lawful cultus, the prescribed place of worship, the priesthood, the kingship. In addition her national existence was blessed by several revivals, notably those under Jehoshaphat; Josiah, and Hezekiah.

Judah was certainly the fundamentalist branch of the chosen people!

From a human point of view, the choice between the two nations is an easy one to make. To us Judah seems more righteous, more spiritual, and more pleasing to God.

But — and here is the real shocker — God says, No. "Backsliding Israel has shown herself to be more righteous than faithless [treacherous] Judah." How could a holy God make such a judgment in view of the facts? The answer is found in the preceding verse. "And even in all these things, unfaithful Judah did not turn to me in full sincerity, but deceitfully, said the Lord." The words of Laetsch are to the point:

> Judah, the treacherous spouse, is like an adulterous wife that seeks to deceive her husband by promising faithfulness while she continues in her relations with other men . . . . Never once did the nation as such return to the Lord wholeheartedly. Their sacrifices were deliberate deception; their weepings, crocodile tears; their hymns, lip service; their avowals of faithfulness, perfidious dissembling . . . Israel was not guiltless. Her wickedness had caused her rejection. Yet as a dirty garment appears cleaner when placed beside a filthy rag, so Israel's undeniable guilt appears less horrible if placed side by side with the guilt of Treachery Judah. God bluntly tells Judah that she has sunk lower than rejected Israel and that she

> is in sore need of returning to the Lord if she hopes to escape a punishment even more severe than that of apostate Israel.[4]

The artificial fruit has a certain temporary beauty. It fools people some of the time, but God is not taken in by it.

In the present context of goodness, hypocrisy is a certain kind of benevolence which is done for selfish reasons, and not out of compassion for people in their need. The outstanding example of that is Ananias and Sapphira whose goodness extended no farther than the impression they wanted to make on the early Christian community. What they had, they were free to dispose of as they wished. But when they tried to make a show of their "goodness," their deceit was exposed and they suffered the extreme penalty. They had not learned the lesson of Jeremiah 3!

The Fruit to Be Cultivated

Of all the fruit of the Spirit, "goodness" is the one which seems to be more exclusively an attribute of God. Jesus detected superficiality in the young ruler's speech when the latter called Him, "Good master" (Luke 18:18). He did not deny that the word applied to Him, but He wanted the young man to see that "good" in the absolute sense can be applied only to God. So He asked him, "Why do you call me good? No one is good except God." A man can be good only in a relative sense.

And yet the relative sense is true goodness also, and it is a reflection of God's goodness which is communicated to us in our regeneration. It is in this relative sense that Barnabas was called a good man in Antioch.

"Goodness" seems to have two senses, and in both senses the word well describes the character of a renewed man. It implies that he was "faultless," and "outgoing."

Faultlessness is perhaps best seen in Daniel's behavior as a member of the court of King Darius. The latter wanted to set Daniel over his whole kingdom, and this stirred up the envy of the other members of government so that they determined to find some cause for his removal from office and from the favor of Darius. Probably they had impeachment in mind. But Daniel was "faithful" in the discharge of his public and personal affairs, and his enemies failed in that attempt to have him removed.

It was only in Daniel's religious life that they hoped to find any fault. But to accomplish this, they had to pass a rule which would make Daniel's particular religion illegal!

Here we see Daniel's "goodness": maturity of character, a devotion to duty, fidelity in the carrying out of his duties. In Pauline terms, he was a man of "good reputation, well thought of by those outside, lest he become involved in slander and fall into the devil's trap" (1 Tim. 3:7).

It may seem paradoxical that a Christian will suffer reproach from the world; that he is to beware when men speak well of him (Luke 6:26); and that he should at the same time have a good reputation among those outside the church. But we must distinguish between the popularity which comes from compromise, and the testimony of goodness which the world sometimes gives despite itself. Daniel's goodness forced a testimony, however grudgingly given. The false prophets Jesus spoke about in Luke 6 bought their popularity by evil speaking.

Goodness is also an outgoing spirit. Men sometimes speak disparagingly of "do-gooders," but what the world needs is many more of them. "Doing good" is a characteristic of God. When the Lycaonians reacted to Paul's miracle with the intention to worship and sacrifice to Barnabas and him, Paul restrained the crowd by calling attention to the apostles' sinful passions (Acts 14:15ff) which rendered them unworthy of any homage, and contrasting them with the living God who "did good and gave you fruitful seasons, filling your hearts with food and gladness."

Jesus urges us to be like His Father: "Love your enemies, and do them good, and lend, not expecting a return; and your reward shall be great, and you shall be sons of the Most High" (Luke 6:35). The world should be a better, happier place because Christians are in it. Notice what these verses, when combined, teach about Christian conduct.

1. God gave them fruitful seasons despite the disobedience of men — so we should not be turned off by men's sinfulness but persevere in deeds of beneficence.

2. We should lend, not expecting a return — the level of poverty should be lower where there are concentrations of Christians.

In the Old Testament the Israelite set aside two tithes — one for the tribe of Levi and the sanctuary, one for the poor. The latter was set aside so that the Israelite would always have something on hand to give to the hungry and the needy. The New Testament counterpart of this must be the deacon's fund in our churches and our own personal charity. It is not only the Christian's presence that should make this a better world to live in, it is also his money, effort, time, and abilities dedicated to the amelioration of his neighbors' conditions and to showing them the true goodness of God.

The Means to Cultivate This Fruit

Paul says that we are re-created "after God" (Eph. 4:24). That is, just as we were originally created "in his image and after his likeness," so once again God uses Himself as the model for our new character. Since God is good, the new man in Christ is good; goodness is part of the Spirit's fruit in him. But the appearance of the fruit in our relations with others is not automatic. To be good, to do good, requires determination, effort, and understanding.

In Romans 15:14, Paul says that his readers were "full of goodness, filled with all knowledge, able also to admonish one another." He had real confidence in them: their goodness and knowledge had advanced to such a degree that mutual criticism could be carried on for the benefit of all. What Paul seems to be saying is this: it takes goodness to give beneficial criticism; it takes goodness to receive it and put it to salutary use; and the result of such criticism, thus given and thus received, will be greater goodness within the Christian community.

It is not easy for a man to see the evil of his own actions. There are many reasons for this: he is not really objective in his thinking; he does all he can to preserve his self-image; the long habits of evil action have become so familiar that they seem good and proper now. So how will he see the evil, to turn from it, and embrace the good? On the human level, one powerful way is to hear, accept, and apply what his fellow Christians say in criticism.

Remember how Abigail, by tactful reproach, saved David from murder? Said David: "As the Lord God of Israel lives, who has withheld me from hurting you, except you had hurried and come to meet me, surely there would not have been left by dawn so much as one child" (1 Sam. 25:34).

Remember how Paul, by open rebuke, delivered Peter from cowardice and from frustrating the impact of the Gospel at Antioch (cf. p. 39)?

The church today is full of potentially good people whose goodness will blossom when the beneficial effects of Christian criticism stir them to activity. This is one of the means God has given us to cultivate goodness.

Questions for Chapter 10

1. Can you name any "good" people today? If so, defend your choices by stating what their characteristics are.
2. Study the account of Barnabas' visit in Antioch (Acts 8). Is there a connection between his character and the results in evangelism? What does this teach us regarding the effectiveness of the fruit in evangelism?
3. We sometimes link being good with being an "easy mark" or a "soft touch." Can a "good" man ever take a strong stand for anything?
4. If God is good, how can He punish anyone? How can He allow wars, famine, disease, etc.?
5. How is goodness related to the other fruit?

Notes

[1] E. J. Young, in *Encyclopedia of Christianity,* Vol. I, p. 285.

[2] Harder in Kittel, *Theological Dictionary of the New Testament,* Vol. VI, p. 557.

[3] *In the Days of His Flesh,* passim.

[4] *Bible Commentary: Jeremiah,* pp. 51f.

Chapter 11

Faithfulness

THE MAN WHO IS CONCERNED only with himself and his own moral rectitude will not have a good reputation for dependability among his neighbors because his actions will be determined by the ebb and flow of his passing moods, not by his commitment to anything outside himself. When the Judaizers turned the Galatians' attentions away from Jesus and to their own works, they robbed them of the possibility of true faithfulness. Faithfulness flows from faith in God.[1] When our attention is focused on Him, a steadiness and dependability develops as His claims and His law govern our actions.

On a small unpretentious tombstone in Greenmount Cemetery in Baltimore are some Greek words. The quotation is from Revelation 2:10, "Faithful unto death." The stone marks the resting-place of the body of J. Gresham Machen. His dependability and integrity showed itself in his scholarly devotion to the truth, in his defense of historic Christianity, and in his perseverance in keeping his ordination vows. He was faithful because he believed in a great God.

THE WEED TO BE ROOTED OUT

Unfaithfulness is un-dependability; that is, the unfaithful

man has no definite direction, no solid supports so that in any given situation we may predict his conduct and therefore have confidence in him.

If we probe a bit deeper, we see that "unfaithfulness" is very close to "disobedience," for the man who disobeys God has cast himself loose from the only solid support a man can have, and his direction in life will be controlled by the shifting winds of circumstances and of his whimsical desires.

In Hebrews the writer says that the Israelites could not enter into Canaan because of "unbelief" (3:19) and "disobedience" (4:6). The unbeliever is disobedient, and the disobedient will be found unfaithful. Hence the terms are interchangeable.

The man who is not controlled by God has no settled reason to keep his word or to discharge his obligations. Because the Old Testament word (from which our "amen" is derived) can be translated both as "truth" and as "faithfulness," the faithful person and the honest man, the unfaithful man and the liar, are frequently identified. Thus Proverbs 12:22 says, "Lying lips are an abomination to the Lord; but they that deal truly [i.e. with faithfulness] are his delight." Delitzsch calls attention to a Jewish proverb: "The lie has no feet (on which it can stand)."[2]

The general lack of faithfulness in our days has resulted in the multiplying of laws, governmental bureaus to enforce those laws, and higher costs of commodities to cover losses due to public tolerance of unfaithfulness. Think how much lower our income taxes would be if the IRS did not have to have such a large staff and complex equipment just to make sure that our returns are trustworthy! And of course the same is true of the Immigration Service, the Department of Agriculture, ad infinitum. The rise of prices due to inflation should not blind us to the accompanying rise of the cost of our infidelity. And the cynicism of our young people today arises largely from the unfaithfulness which they see in the respected and prim older generation.

But unfaithfulness is most heinous when it appears in the Christian community. Yet in many Christian circles a man's word, or his vow is little regarded because there are too many examples of unfaithfulness. Liberals, in the '30's, clung to their pulpits even after they could no longer with honesty quote the Apostles' Creed. But Fundamentalists just as blatantly taught contrary to the historic creeds of their denominations, explaining away what the confessions explicitly taught, though they had vowed to "receive and adopt" them. While the sins of the former were more heinous than those of the latter, the charge of unfaithfulness could not be dodged by either party.

The Artificial Fruit to Be Detected

Outward conformity paid off in Malachi's day, just as it does in our day. Just so long as we use the right words, do the accepted thing! But half-heartedness which is the spring of outward conformity makes God sick. And notice what He does about it! "I will throw dung in your faces" (2:3). Not a nice picture of God, but then the Bible never calls Him nice. It calls Him holy, righteous, and majestic.

Malachi reports a dialogue or debate between God and His people. Let us recall who they were. They were descendants of those who had spent a lifetime in exile because of their disobedience to God's commands. Now released from captivity, the new generation at first revived the true worship and set about building their nation again. But soon the claims of other things — their houses, their business — took precedence over their obligations to God. They began to look for ways of worship which would not entail the great expense which the books of Moses called for.

So, instead of animals "without blemish," they brought lame and sickly animals for sacrifice; instead of freshly baked bread, they left the show-bread to become moldy on the table in the holy place.

God reacted with scornful sarcasm, "Why not take this to your governor? Will he receive you, or do you a favor because you gave him a dinner like this?" (1:8).

He concluded: "Cursed be the cheater who has a healthy

ram in his flock and yet sacrifices an animal with blemishes to the Lord; for I am a great King, says the Lord, and my Name is terrible among the nations" (1:14).

Let's apply this: the Sunday school teacher who hastily prepares the lesson late on Saturday night; the preacher who superficially finds three points in a text and adds three stories; the choir which settles for running over Sunday's selection just once; the "A" student who is content with a "C"; the pastor who is more concerned with the number of calls he makes than with the progress in grace his congregation is making; the Christian who settles for a smile Sunday morning, when a word of encouragement would do so much good; the individual who measures his allegiance to Christ by the number of meetings he attends, instead of by the fruit of the Spirit — to all of these God says, "I will throw dung in your faces," for half-heartedness makes God sick (cf. Rev. 3:16).

The Fruit to Be Cultivated

When we were speaking of the weed of unfaithfulness, we mentioned the prevalence of, and the condoning of, unfaithfulness in our modern economic system. It is interesting to see what can happen when the Holy Spirit has His way in a community. When Joash commanded that offerings be taken for the repair of the temple (2 Kings 12), a sense of integrity pervaded the workmen's actions. "No accounting was required of the men into whose hands they had placed the money, because they dealt honestly" (v. 15). Although we should not desire faithfulness because of its economic returns, we cannot but long for such days.

We do desire faithfulness because it is what God desires. Jesus criticized the Pharisees because of their stress on outward conformity to the exclusion of "the weightier matters of the law, justice, mercy, and faithfulness. These outward acts [tithing and the like] you should have done, and not left the others undone" (Matt. 23:23). God looks for faithfulness among the children of men and grants the seed of it to His own people.

In fact, we may say that without faithfulness we cannot be called the children of God. David describes the citizen of Zion in Psalm 15: "He speaks the truth in his heart. . . . He swears to his own hurt and changes not." The faithfulness God has worked in His children is something of which the world knows nothing. It is an attachment to truth, a determination to persevere in it, that will not be shaken even when it is apparent that it will hurt the pocketbook, or will interfere with one's pleasure, or will mean the loss of an opportunity for personal advancement.

Timothy must have been such a man. When Paul was in prison, his heart went out to the new converts in Philippi. He determined to send someone who could minister in his place and would bring back an accurate account of the Philippians' spiritual condition (Phil. 2:19ff). As Paul went over the names of possible emissaries, he could find only one. The rest were too much taken up with their own affairs, not the things of Jesus Christ.[3]

But Timothy was different. His concern for the Philippians would be genuine, not a phony professional "bedside manner." Timothy would treat them as people, hear their problems, and bear their burdens. Timothy's faithfulness had already been tested and demonstrated in his working with Paul. It was unthinkable that anything would divert his attention from the task assigned him once he had agreed to undertake it.

But the best example of faithfulness in Scripture is that of God Himself. "God is faithful . . . " is a familiar and favorite expression in the New Testament. In Psalm 89, in days when men who walked by sight might have every reason to question God's integrity and dependability, we have one of the clearest expositions of this aspect of God's character. Let us look at some of these:

God's faithfulness is not peripheral, or occasional: the very being of God is to be faithful (v. 8).

God's faithfulness is combined with His power and love, so that no obstacle can arise which might divert Him from His determination to bless His people (vv. 2, 8, 14, 24).

God's faithfulness is in the heavens, and therefore is not subject to changes which occur in the world and to the whims of men of the world (vv. 2, 5).

God's faithfulness is not just His steadiness (like that of the sturdy oak) but is active, reaching out into the affairs of men to help those who have put their trust in Him (v. 24).

God's faithfulness is to His covenant; He has gone the limit of committing His plans to writing so that men of all nations and cultures can read of it and test His fidelity (vv. 3, 5, 28).

God's faithfulness is not contradicted by His decision to wait a long time before He actively honors His promises to His people. The Psalmist closes his song (and indeed Book III of the Psalter) with a doxology which expresses his confidence in the covenant-keeping God.

God's faithfulness is not contradicted by another's faithlessness. Just as Moses interceded for sinning Israel by invoking the names of Abraham, Isaac, and Jacob (Ex. 32:13), so the Psalmist invokes the name of David as he intercedes for sinning Israel many centuries later — he still expected God to honor the covenant even though Israel had proved faithless (vv. 30-37, 49).

God's faithfulness is not obscured when He chastens His people (v. 33). In fact, it is in His faithfulness that He corrects: "I know, O Lord, that your judgments are right, and that you in faithfulness have afflicted me" (Ps. 119:75).

But this review of the faithfulness of God should only serve to remind us that some reflection of His dependability should be present in us.

Our faithfulness should not be peripheral, or occasional. We should not allow circumstances to keep us from our determination to be a blessing among men. In our faithfulness we should reach out to others, and like Timothy, have a concern for their welfare.

Above all, our sense of dependability should not rest on another's faithfulness, and cease when he is found unfaithful. Our faithfulness must have a hidden reserve which continues long after visible supports of it are gone.

Finally, our faithfulness, like God's, should extend to

discipline. "Faithful are the wounds of a friend" (Prov. 27:6). On this last verse, Delitzsch writes: "This, then, is the contrast, that the strokes inflicted by one who truly loves us, although they tear into our flesh . . . , yet are faithful; on the contrary, the enemy covers over with kisses him to whom he wishes all evil."[4] He also cites Psalm 141:5:

> Let the righteous smite me; it shall be a kindness: and let him reprove me; it shall be an excellent oil, which shall not break my head: for yet my prayer also shall be in their calamities.

The Means to Cultivate This Fruit

We must, as God's stewards, be faithful (1 Cor. 4:2). But how shall we cultivate the seed of faithfulness which is ours by regeneration? Perhaps a few suggestions are in order:

1. As we said above, there is *a correlation between obedience and faithfulness*. When we determine to obey the Word of God, we shall be faithful in our actions. This is not only so because we have set obedience as our aim, but also because the Scriptures are a means of grace and our meditation on them produces the fruit of faithfulness: "I have chosen the way of faithfulness: your ordinances I have set before me" (Ps. 119:30).

2. There is *a correlation between our attitude toward God and faithfulness*. Jehoshaphat said to the Levites who were appointed to handle disputes among the people and to apply the Scriptures to them: "Thus shall you do in the fear of the Lord, faithfully, and with a perfect heart" (2 Chron. 19:9). The Old Testament word "fear" carries with it the thought of adoration in addition to the sense of awe and dread. The "fear of the Lord" drives out all other fears, but it leaves the worshiper in awe and wonder, with a sense of purpose and attention to duty which makes him a faithful steward.

3. There is *a correlation between our sense of the significance of the Gospel and faithfulness*. In Titus 2, Paul was urging his readers, who came from many strata of society, to live lives of godliness. When he came to servants (v. 10), he urged them not to steal from their employers, but to demonstrate their faithfulness "so that they may do credit to

the doctrine of God our Saviour in all respects."[5] The Greek word sometimes translated "adorn" may also bear the meaning "do credit to." It is the word from which "cosmetics" is derived; it means "make beautiful or attractive," and the Gospel is made beautiful when men demonstrate its power by their faithfulness. But if we are not particularly impressed by the importance of the Gospel, we shall not be very faithful in the performance of any of our duties!

4. There is *a correlation between our sense of the reality of Christ's coming and our faithfulness*. In Matthew 24:45ff, Jesus contrasts the "faithful and wise servant" with the "evil servant." The former is obediently following instructions when the master comes and is rewarded for his faithfulness. The latter does not take the Lord's return seriously and is punished for his faithlessness.

In the so-called Parable of the Talents (Matt. 25:14ff) two of the servants were found faithful to their trust and they entered into the joy of the Lord. For their faithfulness, they were entrusted with great responsibility. But the unfaithful servant was called "wicked and slothful" and he was thrown into outer darkness.

These admonitions should bear upon the consciences of Christians today. There has been a revulsion against eschatological studies because of excesses committed in the past by superficial and careless students of the Bible. But there can be no revulsion against the plain teachings of the Scriptures — that when Jesus returns, He will test men according to their faithfulness. The Bible does not teach carnal security — it teaches that faithfulness is an indispensable mark of a Christian. Without it the Christian's testimony is only hypocritical.

Questions for Chapter 11

1. List the ways unfaithfulness appears in your life, your family, your church or Christian organization.
2. Is it worthwhile to be faithful when so many people are not dependable? If so, why?

3. Why are "obedience" and "faithfulness" so clearly related?
4. Do you think it is nice for God to use such words as "dung," and to threaten such actions as, "I will throw dung in your faces"?
5. When was the last time you, as a faithful friend, inflicted wounds on someone you love?
6. Study the verse, "If we are faithless, he remains faithful; for he cannot deny himself" (2 Tim. 2:13). Does this deny "eternal security"?
7. How is faithfulness related to the other fruit?

Notes

[1] Indeed the Greek word *pistis* is translated by both "faith" and "faithfulness." The King James Version has "faith" among the fruit of the Spirit. However, I prefer "faithfulness" since Galatians 5 is dealing with traits of character produced in men of faith by the Holy Spirit and made evident in interpersonal relationships. There is a special function of faith such as that referred to in 1 Corinthians 12, 13, but there is no evidence that this is in view in Galatians 5.

[2] *Biblical Commentary on the Proverbs of Solomon,* Vol. I, p. 263.

[3] Some who would glorify "the early church" should keep verses like this in mind. There were only a few carrying the burden and yet the job was done.

[4] *Biblical Commentary on the Proverbs of Solomon,* Vol. II, p. 202.

[5] This translation is suggested by Arndt and Gingrich, *op. cit.,* p. 446.

Chapter 12

Meekness and Gentleness

IN A CERTAIN SENSE, Peter's temporary lapse (narrated in Galatians 2) was a portrait in miniature of the present state of the Galatians. In a moment of fear, he lapsed into the Judaizers' error and thus earned Paul's rebuke. But which came first, the fear or the lapse? As we read the closing verses of chapter 2, it appears that Paul's diagnosis was: a vagueness in understanding the doctrine of grace made Peter afraid. Similarly, Paul's clear grasp of "grace" made him courageous despite the enmity it aroused on every hand. "Fear" and "courage" are symptoms of our inward state.

Have you noticed the absense of such an important virtue as "courage" from the list of the fruit of the Spirit? In fact, some people imagine that courage is not a Christian virtue at all, but that Caspar Milquetoast is the true picture of a Christian. As a matter of fact, as we shall see, Caspar Milquetoast is an artificial fruit, a carnal compromise which is neither the self-seeking weed born of the flesh, nor the meekness born of the Spirit.

Meekness and gentleness are not the opposites of courage; it takes courage to be meek and gentle in an evil world.

Meekness is the opposite of self-seeking, and it is to this latter weed that we must now turn our attention.

The Weed to Be Rooted Out

In Luke 9:46-56 we see a prime illustration of it — a controversy arose among Jesus' disciples, "Which of us is the greatest?" We do not know how this discussion began or what motives lay behind it. It could have been sheer idle talk, mere thoughtless prattle such as we all engage in sometimes. It could have been pride and self-centeredness, which on another occasion provoked a similar discussion (Mark 10:35)![1]

Whatever its character at the beginning, it soon became quite vicious. It developed into an attitude of party-spirit, an attitude which could see the right only on one side and which refused to admit that God could use anyone else (v. 49). In their narrow-mindedness, they could not see their own needs and weaknesses which all too soon became apparent.

Some time later, as the point of the discussion festered within their hearts, violence reared its ugly head and two of their leaders succumbed to it. It came about this way. Jesus was planning ahead for an overnight stand in a Samaritan village. The Samaritans however did not want Jews in their village overnight, particularly any Jews who were headed for the feast at Jerusalem. This was just another example of the long-standing feud between Samaritans and Jews, and the natural enmity of James and John surfaced as they said to Jesus, "Do you want us to command fire to come down from heaven to destroy them?"

Jesus severely rebuked them, and they were probably puzzled about it all. Elijah had done something of the sort (2 Kings 1) and Jesus was greater than Elijah. The disciples had received power to work miracles, and they thought that this would be a good time to use that authority again.

In their reasoning they failed to see their place in redemptive history. All the events of the Scriptures have a place in God's program, but God does not always work in the same way in different periods of history. Elijah did well to call fire from heaven for he lived in a day of apostasy and it was God's will that apostasy be punished as the Israelites of the northern kingdom were carried away by the Assyrians. Elijah's act was to be a symbol of impending judgment, even as it was also a type of distant judgment, at the last day.

But the disciples were not on the verge of judgment; they were on the threshhold of a great surge of evangelism which would bring many of these very Samaritans to the knowledge of the truth (cf. John 4:21; Acts 8:5ff).

But their self-centeredness had begotten party-spirit, and party-spirit, vengeance. They had forgotten the meaning of "the Gospel," the good news, and the significance of Jesus' words, "The son of man is come not to call the righteous, but sinners to repentance."

The time for fire will come, and when it is called down it will be sent down in righteousness, not selfishness.

The weed of self-centeredness embitters, blinds, and frustrates the grace of God. It is a noxious weed, and Jesus rebuked His disciples severely for it.

The Artificial Fruit to Be Detected

But if not self-centeredness, party-spirit, and violence, then what? Surely their opposites — false modesty, self-depreciation, and spineless refusal to stand for anything!

This artificial fruit denies one's personhood, one's God-given abilities and talents. God has given every man some gift, so every man is worthwhile in God's eyes. This is not to deny our sinful depravity or our true guilt before God. But it is to assert that even the lowest person has a dignity, a value, and a uniqueness because he was made in God's image. Now the artificial fruit denies all this, and dehumanizes the individual so that he is no longer what God intended him to be.

This artificial fruit is not true virtue. It is a cowardly retreat from reality which substitutes a passive selfishness, and only avoids trouble at the cost of allowing even greater trouble to develop.

We see examples of this on every hand: the speaker who has just given an excellent speech, who mutters, "It was nothing"; the soloist who has real ability to sing, who pushes it all aside with, "I'm just getting over a cold." It is the refusal to recognize that God has given us abilities and has given successes as we have used them.

I once spoke with a missionary who had decided not to return to the field. As we spoke, it became evident that returning was the one thing she really wanted to do, and in fact for that reason she had decided not to! She had been told that the Christian must deny himself every desire, no matter what it might be. And in her case, since her greatest desire was to return to the mission field, she must suppress it for God's sake. She was certainly a miserable young lady.

Thus the artificial fruit is really lying — to ourselves and to others. It is perhaps a natural reaction to pride and boasting, but it is just as ugly as the weed, for it denies God's place in our lives.

Far better is the advice of Susanna Wesley, the mother of John and Charles, who was equally concerned with meekness and modesty. She counseled men not to praise children because of their natural talents — the beauty of a little girl, the natural athletic prowess of a little boy. Her approach was to say something like this to the girl, "Hasn't God given you pretty curls?" and to the boy, "Wasn't it good of the Lord to give you a fine body?"

Here was perfect honesty: The acceptance of ourselves as we really are, as God has endowed us with His gifts; but also the full recognition that we are what we are only because He has created us, and has given us gifts of grace.

False modesty denies all this, and Christians should be aware of its heinous character and of God's feelings toward it.

The Fruit to Be Cultivated

Just as self-centeredness produces violence, so meekness produces gentleness. At our regeneration the Spirit planted within us the seed of accepting ourselves for what we really are, and this seed will blossom into meekness and gentleness.

The Bible says that Moses excelled in meekness. In fact it is Moses who tells us that! The description came at a time when Miriam and Aaron were rebelling against the place of leadership occupied by their younger brother. Delitzsch's remarks are to the point: "No one approached Moses in meekness, because no one was raised so high by God as he was. The higher the position which a man occupies among his fellow men, the harder it is for the natural man to bear attacks upon himself with meekness, especially if they are directed against his official rank and honor. This remark as to the character of Moses serves to bring out to view the position of the person attacked, and points out the reason why Moses not only abstained from all self-defense, but did not even cry to God for vengeance on account of the injury that had been done to him. Because he was the meekest of all men, he could calmly leave this attack upon himself to the all-wise and righteous Judge, who had both called and qualified him for his office."[2] Delitzsch later quotes from Calmet, "As he praises himself here without pride, so he will blame himself elsewhere with humility"; and then Delitzsch calls Moses, "a man of God whose character is not to be measured by the standard of ordinary men."[3]

Meekness arises from an understanding of ourselves, and it gives us insight into the needs of others. Paul describes the Lord's servant as one who "must not quarrel, but must be gentle to everyone, able to teach, bearing evil without resentment, with meekness teaching those who oppose themselves, with the hope that God would give to them repentance and a full knowledge of the truth, and that they would escape from the devil's trap in which they have been held captive, so that they will from now on do God's will" (2 Tim. 2:24ff).

In this context, meekness helps us to understand what people do to themselves when they sin: they oppose themselves; and we understand also why they do this: they are caught in a trap.

Our daily lives are full of conflicts with people. When they become obstacles in our way, we are prone to react with some degree of violence against them. Usually the degree of our violence is in direct proportion to our insecurity and instability. Insecurity often comes from an unwillingness to accept reality, and meekness helps to cure our insecurity.

In fact, when we truly understand ourselves, there are no limits toward which we will not go to help others. When Jesus heard the disciples arguing about their relative greatness, He placed a child before them and told them to help him. True greatness is meekness — to be concerned with the needs of a child.

Now meekness, seen in this light, is not a common commodity. It is so different from what people do, and expect others to do, that it takes real courage to be meek.

But will meekness work? And will gentleness carry the day? The answer to this question is to be found in one of the prophecies which Isaiah makes of Messiah, and which Matthew recalls as he describes Jesus' refusal to become a popular figure among the people (Matt. 12:15). Many people followed Jesus after He healed the man with the withered hand, and all of them who had diseases were likewise healed by Him. What a surge of enthusiasm there must have been as each healing took place.[4]

But Jesus warned them not to speak about Him publicly. Matthew, as he thought about it, was reminded of the Isaiah passage, and he quoted it fully: "Behold my servant whom I have chosen, my beloved in whom my soul is well pleased: I will put my Spirit upon him, and he shall declare judgment to the Gentiles. He shall not strive or cry aloud, neither shall any one hear his voice in the streets. A bruised reed he will not break, and a smoking flax he will not quench, till he send forth judgment unto victory. And in his name will the Gentiles hope" (42:1-4).

Here we see real meekness and gentleness set before us in human flesh by the Son of God. Again we quote from Delitzsch: "Although He is certain of His divine call, and brings to the nations the highest and best, His manner of appearing is nevertheless quiet, gentle, and humble; the very opposite of those lying teachers, who endeavored to exalt themselves by noisy demonstrations. He does not seek His own, and therefore denies Himself; He brings what commends itself, and therefore requires no forced trumpeting."[5] This is meekness, the quiet awareness of who He is, and of the power He has at His disposal for the accomplishment of His ends.

Now His awareness of His power enables Him to be gentle to those in need. Isaiah uses two figures of speech. The first is that of a cracked, half-broken reed. It will part in two forever under the rough treatment of men in the world.

In Jesus' hands the reed will not be further broken; in fact, it will be fully restored. When Jesus is at hand, no one is beyond hope, no matter how hopeless he may believe his lot to be.

The second is that of a flickering, almost extinguished wick. A sudden movement will quench the light entirely. But in Jesus' hands, the flame will be safe for He will be gentle and understanding.

We have seen how "meekness" is related to "gentleness." But our question still remains, "Will they work?" Isaiah says they will. "He will really bring forth righteousness. He will not fail nor be discouraged until he has set justice in the earth" (42:4).

Meekness and gentleness are not signs of weakness. They are strong, and are powerful weapons in God's hands to accomplish His purposes. They require courage on the part of the one exercising them, and also great faith that God will use them as He has promised. But the fact is that sin has so bruised the human spirit that such tender treatment is required if those spirits are to be made whole again. In these days of coldness and hatred among people, it is particularly necessary that Christians learn gentleness.

The Means to Cultivate This Fruit

In a verse which immediately precedes the Matthew passage (12:12) we discussed above, Jesus made a remark which is intended to teach us meekness and gentleness. He said,

"How much then is a man of more value than a sheep?" (v. 12). If you were given a piece of cut glass so expensive as to make it irreplaceable, how carefully and how gently you would handle it! Human life is so much more valuable and precious. How valuable? It can only be valued by the price tag God placed on it — "He gave his only begotten Son." We must recall this the next time we are tempted to treat another person roughly.

But tenderness and gentleness must come from within. It springs from that estimate of ourselves which makes us meek, and that estimate must come from the Scriptures.

1. *We are creatures who have obligations to our Creator*. Acknowledgment of this will keep us from self-centeredness and pride.

2. *We are sinners who have lost our rights*. The position grace has bestowed on us is an exalted one until we let it go to our heads. Then we tend to lord it over each other and become violent in our relations. But grace teaches tenderness when we recall what we really deserve.

3. *We are incapable of good apart from God*. The world can do what men call "good," and often Christians settle for that level of goodness and congratulate themselves upon attaining it. But the goodness God requires is something else, and it is humbling to realize how frail and impotent we are.

4. *We are saved for a purpose*. Says Paul in Romans 6, salvation is a change of masters. We never get out from under bondage and obligations. Our new bondage is fulfilled when we realize why God saved us: "You are bought with a price; therefore glorify God. . . ." And God is glorified when we "show forth the virtues of him who has called us out of darkness. . . ." One of these virtues is gentleness.

5. *We are being trained for a purpose*. God brings into our lives experiences which will give opportunity for us to grow in meekness and gentleness. These experiences are often meaningless apart from this truth. Moses was trained for eighty years (not wasted years as he later looked back on them) so that he could be the meekest man of his day.

6. *We are empowered to fulfill that purpose*. We have so

little power, it seems. But God promises us power similar to that which raised Jesus from the dead (Eph. 1:19). We will discover the power when we discover the purpose. In other words, there is plenty of power to make us meek, and we will see it operating within us when we set our sights on the One who is truly meek.

Questions for Chapter 12

1. Jesus said, "Blessed are the meek, for they shall inherit the earth" (Matt. 5:5). He seems to be quoting Psalm 37:11. Study these verses together. Do they refer to the eternal state, or are they a present promise? Or may they refer to both? Give reasons for whatever position you take.
2. How can we avoid falling into the sin of "party-spirit"?
3. Can you think of some examples which show the power of meekness?
4. Suppose gentleness "doesn't work"? Should we continue in it?
5. What is the best way to help an arrogant person to see his error?
6. How are meekness and gentleness related to the other fruit?

Notes

[1] The total thoughtlessness and self-centeredness is apparent when we consider the larger context of these verses. Jesus had just announced His crucifixion (v. 44) and instead of dwelling on that, they sink into a discussion of *their* greatness!

[2] *Biblical Commentary on the Pentateuch,* Vol. III, p. 77.

[3] *Ibid.*, p. 78.

[4] Warfield in *Miracles: Yesterday and Today, Real and Counterfeit*, comments: "The number of the miracles which He wrought may easily be underrated. It has been said that in effect He banished disease and death from Palestine for the three years of His ministry. If this is exaggeration, it is pardonable exaggeration" (p. 3).

[5] *Biblical Commentary on the Prophecies of Isaiah,* Vol. II, p. 175.

Chapter 13

Self-control

AMONG THE "WORKS of the flesh" in Galatians 5:19-21, Paul lists several instances of a lack of self-control: "unrestrainedness," "drunkenness," "carousings." But there are many, many types of lack of self-control.

When Nehemiah heard that the walls of Jerusalem were broken down and its gates destroyed by fire, his face fell and he was sick at heart. Although he had known for some time that the city had been in ruins, the report of its broken-down walls seemed to break his spirit.

Broken walls are a symbol of final collapse. A city without walls in ancient times had lost all its defenses and its identity. It was prey to every kind of enemy, natural as well as human. And when this happened to the city of God, it was a calamity indeed!

Solomon likened an undisciplined spirit to a city in such a state of collapse (Prov. 16:32; 25:28). The lack of self-control is a calamity greater than that of a city destroyed because it means that an eternal soul has reached a final state of decay.

The Weed to Be Rooted Out

Basically, the weed seems to be a habit of choosing continually something bad or harmful rather than something good; or a continual choosing of a lesser good in preference to something more important.

1. *An Uncontrollable Body*

According to Paul an example of lack of self-control is excess of eating or drinking. Eating and drinking are not evil, but their excess becomes evil. Lack of self-control can be like worshiping a false god. In Philippians 3:18f, Paul says of those who abuse their Christian liberty in eating, that their "god is the belly," and for that reason they will end in destruction—that of which they once boasted, they will soon be ashamed.

Paul's argument is similar to the sermons of the prophets, especially Isaiah. For just as idol-worshipers in the Old Testament were enemies of the God of Israel, so those who lack self-control are enemies of the cross of Christ. Moreover, just as the idol worshipers sooner or later discovered that their god was unable to help them, so the abuser of his body discovers that his god has also brought him to shame.

Paul carries this parallel even further in Ephesians 5:18ff. There is an analogy between drunkenness and being filled with the Spirit. In each case the individual gives up the control and domination of his life to another—in the case of the drunkard, alcohol, in the case of the Christian, the Spirit of God. This is why excess in drinking is so heinous: it places a beverage where only God ought to be!

But it will not last long. In wine is "dissipation" or "debauchery," Paul says. The adjective describes the prodigal son's life after he left home ("riotous living," Luke 15:13). Literally, the word means "past redemption" or "without hope." These verses teach us that whenever we, in a lack of self-discipline, hand over our lives to the control of anything except the living God, we will land in utter ruin and shame. Such lack of self-control in regard to the body is a violation of the sixth commandment, and for such a trespass an unbeliever will be condemned (cf. Col. 3:5, 6).

In 1 Corinthians 6, Paul adds a reason for rooting the weed out of the Christian — since the body is now a sanctuary of the Holy Spirit, to injure the body is an affront to Him.

2. *An Uncontrollable Spirit*

But self-control should be extended over a much wider area than the body. The "undisciplined spirit" mentioned by the Proverbs shows itself in anger, envy, and covetousness.

Now while these sins themselves are frequently condemned and judged by God, they have a peculiarity which makes them even more heinous — they open the door to every other kind of offense because the spirit has no defenses left against them. We return to the illustration of the city in ruins. Every kind of marauder is free to roam, to pollute, and to carry away. So an uncontrollable spirit is never alone because it welcomes sins of every kind to dwell within. Thus, Moses' anger against the people led him to tempt God, and for this second offense he was denied entrance to Canaan (cf. Num. 20:10ff; 27:13; Deut. 1:37). The envy of the Jews' rulers opened the door to the false accusations against Jesus, His crucifixion, and all the evils attendant upon it. Ahab's covetousness opened the door to Naboth's murder and the confiscation of his vineyard.

In each of these instances, lack of self-control led the individual to strike out after a lesser good, and in that pursuit he committed crimes which in sober moments he might have refused to commit. Self-control would have counseled patience till the primary value might have been gained.

The Artificial Fruit to Be Detected

Let me make this seeking of the "lesser good" concrete. I once heard two former alcoholics give their testimonies against the evils of intemperance. One of them had evidently been helped to sobriety by all sorts of psychological gimmicks, and she was now sustaining herself by a series of gimmicks. In particular she found support by laughing at herself in her former condition; and the more she could laugh, the more she determined not to return to that state. It was funny; we all laughed with her. But then somehow it no longer seemed funny. It was pitiful in the long view, and most of us stopped laughing. She laughed on because she had to — it was her only resource. Little did it matter that in the process she lost her personhood and was only the butt of a joke. But instead of destroying herself by the bottle, she was withering away as something merely to be laughed at.

Now achieving temperance this way is only a lesser good because God has something better for us, and we were introduced to the grace of God by the next speaker who spoke quite plainly and simply of her release from the bondage of alcohol through the power of Jesus Christ. Here was a real person, accepting both her past and her present as real, and content with the better thing which she had chosen in Jesus Christ.

Jesus describes this artificial fruit in vivid but terrifying language in Luke 11:24-26. In His audience were some people who were impressed by His works and they were believing on Him — they were choosing a real good. Others were not impressed at all and were hostile to Him. These were those who later on would for envy turn Him over to the authorities for crucifixion. But there was the inevitable third group who were trying to be neutral, not perhaps ascribing Beelzebub's power to Him, but neither also were they ready to embrace Him as the Messiah. They did not envy Him, and so at the moment were not guilty of a lack of self-control; but Jesus says that their attempt at neutrality would open the door to the grossest of sins.

Jesus likened them to someone who had resisted an evil spirit but who was not ready to choose Jesus Christ as the primary object of his affection. So the spirit which had been cast out returned to fill the vacuum and brought with him seven other spirits more wicked than he.

There is a sort of self-control which can reject a particular sinful act; but if that self-control refuses the grace of God, the result is really only trading one sin for another, and the latter will be worse than the former. Thus does Jesus rebuke preaching which is negative only, a preaching which calls on people to give up this or that evil habit but never confronts the sinner with Jesus Christ and His claims. We must not be taken in by the artificial fruit; we must seek for that self-control which is the gift of God.

The Fruit to Be Cultivated

We exercise control over ourselves when we have some clear ambition or aim. Left to ourselves we will always choose actual evil or lesser good as our goal ("There is none that does good"). The fruit of the Spirit gives us the best of all goals, God's glory, and the power to make progress toward it. This fact is illustrated in Paul's own life, and then in the experience of participants in the Isthmian games.

1. *Paul's Self-control* (Acts 23:1-5)

At first reading, the account does not seem to vindicate Paul's self-control. In response to a slap on the mouth, Paul raised his voice indignantly, "God will hit you, you white-washed wall."

Paul was being examined at what we would call today a pretrial hearing. The Sanhedrin met at the order of the Roman tribune to see if there really was a case against Paul. If there was, then the Sanhedrin would meet later as the trial court. So "Paul had not yet been properly charged, let alone tried and found guilty."[1] Under Jewish law, he was innocent until he was found guilty. The hypocrisy of the highpriest was evident, and to call him a "white-washed wall" was no over-statement of the facts.[2]

So what impresses us about Paul is the *instantaneous submission* to the law of God, once he was made aware that the speaker who so unlawfully ordered him to be struck was the high priest. With all the pressures flooding in upon him — the threats of the mob to lynch him, the feeling that he could not get a fair trial, the injustice of the command to hit him — Paul "had the presence of mind" to recall the Exodus command, and instantaneously to control his emotions and apologize to his oppressors: "for it is written, You shall not speak evil of a ruler of your people."

We do not justify all of Paul's actions and reactions as he faced his opponents — he was a man of like passions with us. We do marvel at such self-control which in Paul was a mark of the Spirit's work. "My sheep hear my voice." As soon as Paul heard the voice, every faculty was called into obedience so that his life's aim might here and now find fulfillment — the glory of God.

2. *The Athlete's Self-control* (1 Cor. 9:24ff)

Paul seems to have been impressed by the stamina, the skill, and the temperance of athletes. Their self-control involves an aim, a list of training rules, and constant, sustained effort.

Aim — The athlete runs so he can win a prize (v. 24a). Now some laggards also run, but they don't care about winning a prize (v. 24b). Hence, their self-control is minimal. Whatever temperance they might have had is nullified by the multitude of desires which pull them in every direction. So they never "obtain."

The champion athlete aims for a prize that soon withers — a mere wreath. The Christian has an incorruptible prize: all the greater reason for self-control.

A list of training rules — The champion athlete has an eye for all the rules in his training sheet (v. 25). We can control ourselves in the case of things we really don't want. Temperance becomes a problem when our desires are actively set on some things. It becomes a question of aim. If we really want the prize, we will desire other things less.

The Christian has his training regimen. In fact, 1 Corinthians 8 and 9 is a discussion of such things. The Christian's faithfulness to his training depends on his devotion to the goal he has set before him — "lest by any means, after I have preached to others, I myself should be rejected."

Constant, sustained effort — "I am running . . . I am fighting . . . I am buffeting . . . . " The verbs are present tense. When an athlete trained for the Isthmian games which were held near Corinth, he devoted his full-time to practice. There were of course other things to do — lawful things, good things — but not good enough. So the athlete excluded from his life anything which would harm his body.

When this is applied to the Christian, it will be seen that he is in "full-time service." The fruit of the Spirit which is self-control is not some luxury to be enjoyed by an elite among Christians; it is a reality in the life of everyone who has been claimed by Christ. Hence to be a Christian is to be self-controlled all the time.

We should not misunderstand Paul here. He is not urging a monastic life: self-control is not a withdrawal from the affairs of men. Temperance is the decision to have a well-defined goal, an intelligent manner of life which will make that goal possible, and a continual pressing toward the goal until it is reached.

The Means to Cultivate This Fruit

The Roman Caesar, so the story goes, had a slave as his constant companion, and the slave's duty was to whisper in his monarch's ear — "You are human."

Some such constant reminder is needed if the Christian is to cultivate temperance. But the word "human" is not strong enough. We must hear a greater truth from God, "You are not your own. You are bought with a price" (1 Cor. 6:19, 20).

The Holy Spirit, in our regeneration, has implanted a seed which will flower into temperance. When we are first conscious of our guilt and our need for a Savior, our priorities are usually in good order: "Nothing in my hand I bring, Simply to Thy cross I cling." But in our conscious life we do not always stay with our priorities, and they become confused and lesser goods claim our attention and our devotion. This is why we need a daily reminder of who we are, who God is, where we came from, and where we are headed. With these truths to remind us, we will grow in temperance.

Questions for Chapter 13

1. List some of the "lesser goods" which tempt Christians today.
2. Why does Paul list as a qualification for an elder: "not pugnacious"?
3. How can we help each other in developing self-control?
4. How is self-control related to each of the other fruit?

NOTES

[1] Bruce, *The Book of Acts*, p. 450.
[2] *Op. cit.*, pp. 449-452.

Chapter 14

Putting Faith to Work

IN THE PRECEDING chapters, the point has been made that the Holy Spirit implanted a seed within each Christian at the moment of that person's regeneration, and that as a result of both God's work and the believer's cultivation of that implanted seed, the fruit of the Spirit appears. In each chapter which dealt with the fruit, a section was devoted to the means that are revealed in the Scripture for the cultivation of the fruit.

Further consideration of the subject (and the opportunity to interact with many congregations who had both read the preceding chapters and heard the substance of what is to follow) has led me to develop in greater detail some insights based on Galatians 5:6. The basic diagram is found on p. 16 of this volume. The point that Paul made is this: Faith and love are so integrally related that love is an inevitable result of true faith. Love in turn, as it is shaped and directed by the content of faith, produces the rest of the fruit. Thus our diagram may be expanded as follows:

Of course, the view being presented here must not be confused with the Roman Catholic identification of faith and love such that love is the essence of faith, that we are justified on account of love, that love is what makes faith a Christian virtue. We agree with the statement of Charles Hodge, "That love is the invariable and necessary attendant and consequent of saving faith."[1]

This position rests upon the Reformation truth, *sola fide* (by faith alone). Our understanding of the fruit of the Spirit will be enriched if we relate it to the Protestant view of faith. It was said, back in the days of the Reformation, that the Christian world was divided by four letters: *sola*, a Latin word that in English means "alone." The word *sola* was combined with other Latin words to express Reformational truth: *sola Scriptura* (by Scripture alone); *sola gratia* (by grace alone); and *sola fide*.

This word *sola* became important because the Roman Catholic teachers agreed with the Reformers on the importance of Scripture, grace, and faith. The Reformers however insisted, and the Catholics denied, that the Scriptures *alone* are sufficient revelation for the purposes of redemption, and that we are saved by grace and faith *alone* apart from works. The Protestants stressed the need for faith alone because they understood from Scripture that the most important gift one can ever receive from God is the gift of faith. Faith, but faith alone, is the doorway to every blessing promised and provided by our blessed Lord.

This last thought can be illuminated for us in 2 Peter 1. As a preliminary to grasping Peter's thought let me remind you of an experience many of us have had on such special occasions as anniversaries, birthdays, or going-away parties. At an appropriate moment someone presented the guest of honor with a large box, beautifully wrapped and tied with colorful ribbons. The guest pulled off the bow, removed the wrapping paper, and then opened the box. Inside that box was a somewhat smaller box similarly wrapped and adorned with ribbons. When those wrappings were removed, another box appeared and so on, box after box, until the guest arrived at a very small box which contained often a very valuable gift. That experience may help us to understand Peter's point in the first chapter of his second epistle.

In his opening remarks Peter reminded his readers that they had "received a faith of the same kind as ours." We Christians use the word "faith" in two ways. It may refer to the *act* of believing: Jesus said, "Have faith in God" (Mark 11:22). Peter may be saying that he and his readers have received the power to rest upon Jesus Christ *in the same way*. The act of faith was the same for all — God granted the same ability to believe to both apostles and less-gifted saints. In this sense, faith was a great leveler, for all had to come to God through faith and through this act of believing alone.

On the other hand, "faith" was often used for the content of what they believed: Jude urged his readers to "contend earnestly for the faith which was once for all delivered to the saints" (Jude 3). Perhaps Peter was saying that he and his readers had received and rested upon *the same body of truth*. The content of their faith was the same for all — for both the apostle Peter and his readers, whoever they might have been. Again, "faith" leveled them — they, all of them, had to believe the same things.

Indeed, it may not be necessary for us to decide between these alternatives. Commentators may be found on either side of the issue. But, as B. B. Warfield argues,[2] the word "faith" even in the sense of the act of believing "trembles" on the verge of being a synonym for the Christian religion, i.e., the content of our faith. This is so because, after all, the Christian never believes in a vacuum — the believer always believes in God and in what God has revealed. Hence the Spirit empowers us to believe only what He has already revealed. It is "faith" in its twofold aspect that Peter wanted his readers to examine.

In v. 3 he expanded that thought to show that God had "granted to us everything pertaining to life and godliness." Peter wanted to assure his readers that as believers they need lack nothing essential for their walk as pilgrims through the world. In v. 4 he reminded them that God had granted them "his precious and magnificent promises, in order that by them you might become partakers of the divine nature." Here surely the stress is on the content of faith.

The emphasis thus far has been on God's gracious activity in taking the initiative in salvation, but next Peter reminded his readers that human effort was not thereby discouraged. His words, "for this very reason" (v. 5), indicated that God's initiative should be construed by Christians as the best of motivations for living a godly life. So great should this motivation be that Peter commanded his readers to apply *all* diligence. Putting faith to work, which is at the heart of all that we want to say in this chapter, is a matter of the highest priority for the Christian. With diligence, then, Peter said, "In your faith supply moral excellence."

"Supply" is an important word in this passage. In classical Greek it sometimes referred to the furnishing of a chorus in a drama. Some well-to-do person would be asked to give money so that the chorus might have appropriate costumes. It is used in the New Testament in several places ("minister," KJV — 2 Cor. 9:10; Gal. 3:5; Col. 2:19; 2 Peter 1:11). In all but one of these instances, something was supplied *to* someone, but in 2 Peter 1:5 Peter said that something was supplied *in*. Perhaps his meaning can best be expressed by paraphrasing as follows: "Look in your faith for moral excellence; discover in your moral excellence, knowledge; in your knowledge, you will see that self-control is already furnished" and so on.

We will see Peter's meaning now if we relate this paraphrase to the illustration of opening boxes. The first box is "faith," the source of all blessings and fruit in the Christian life. Faith which has united us to Jesus Christ, which has laid hold on all the promises of God — that faith has in it all we need for life and godliness. To discover these resources we must open the boxes, or to change the figure, we must put our faith to work. Believing all the promises of God and counting on the power of the Spirit of God, we will find within that faith, moral excellence.

For example, suppose you have a problem with a quick temper. Someone crosses you, and before you know it, you have "blown your stack." You simply cannot control that temper. Peter says, "Put your faith to work and you will find in that faith the strength to produce, instead of wrath, true godly virtue."

Let us analyze a hot temper to see what Peter is talking about. We become angry when someone says or does something that we do not like or that we think is morally wrong. We are quick to condemn and do so in the power of a very strong emotion. But what does our faith tell us about that other person? More importantly, what does our faith tell us about God? Is He a faraway deity, or the God of providence? Does He have His way "in the host of heaven and among the inhabitants of earth" (Dan. 4:35)? Does He not cause "all things to work together for good to those who love God, to those who are called according to His purpose?" So then, that word or act which caused us such intense anger is actually an event totally within God's control. Now it is a deed done by God as well as by a sinner, and therefore we may view it from two sides. We may concentrate on the human, sinful side and fill our souls with a root of bitterness which will only destroy us; or we may contemplate the wisdom and love of God and fill our souls with joy and moral excellence.

Joseph is the outstanding example of this. Hated by his brothers, betrayed by Potiphar's wife, and forgotten by the chief butler, Joseph had more than enough provocation to wrath, rage, and self-pity. But his words indicate that he put his faith to work and he received his brothers in love and affection: "God sent me before you to preserve life. . . . And God sent me before you to preserve for you a remnant in the earth, and to keep you alive by a great deliverance. . . . You meant evil against me, but God meant it for good in order to bring about this present result, to preserve many people alive. . . . So he comforted them and spoke kindly to them" (Gen. 45:5, 7; 50:20f).

I have stressed the relation between faith and moral excellence, using a hot temper as an example, but the truth applies to many other circumstances. Our faith in God provides us with all the resources we need for virtue, or moral excellence.

It should be stressed that Joseph did more than control himself, as significant as that is. His faith produced *moral excellence*. The same word was used in 1 Peter 2:9: "But you are . . . that you may proclaim the *excellencies* . . . " (italics mine). In his first epistle Peter called his readers to a life of proclamation. Since God had acted so bountifully in saving them (their glory was to be "a chosen race, a royal priesthood, a holy nation, a people for God's own possession"), their response was to proclaim His excellencies. The word is the same in the original. We are tempted therefore to say that the "moral excellence" of 2 Peter 1:5 is *Christlikeness*. When we put our faith to work, we produce not only a negative result (such as controlling a quick temper), but a positive likeness to God. Hencc Joseph not only controlled a tendency to hatred and vengeance, but "comforted them and spoke kindly to them."

Next Peter wrote: Look into your virtue and you will find knowledge. Now "knowledge" is a word with many meanings in the Bible. As Peter used it in this verse, I believe, he wanted us to understand the kind of knowledge that comes from experience — the conviction that since God has worked in our behalf to produce moral virtue, He will continue to do so. It is in this sense that the gift box containing moral excellence contains knowledge.

Peter could speak of this out of his own experience. During the trial of Jesus he was tempted to deny the Savior. He did not put his faith to work and so refused to confess Him;

somehow he did not believe that God could and would take care of him. Later on, in the Book of Acts, Peter spoke out boldly, and God delivered him on several occasions (cf. Acts 5 and 12). In the light of those experiences, Peter could now write with much assurance, not only that God would care for His people during their pilgrim days, but also that He would preserve them to their heavenly home. When he put his faith to work, he found courage; and when he saw that God had worked to give him courage, he discovered an assurance that was new and invigorating.

"In your knowledge, self-control." I have already written at some length about self-control (see chapter 13). More should be said on this subject, however, because Peter indicated to his readers that there is a connection between faith, moral excellence, and experiential knowledge on the one hand, and self-control on the other.

We may see this relation in the lives of two Old Testament kings. Saul was disbelieving, corrupt, and rash. He took matters in his own hands and had a thought for God only when Samuel was present to remind him of his covenant obligations. He was a contrast to David, "a man after [God's] own heart" (1 Sam. 13:14). David believed God, and he was a "better" man than Saul (1 Sam. 15:28). We can only understand "better" as meaning morally or spiritually better. David was not chosen because he had greater administrative abilities than Saul; he was a better man because he had already put his faith to work. His moral excellence gave him knowledge and confidence that God would deliver him from the giant Goliath even as He had delivered him from a lion and a bear. And that knowledge and confidence was what David needed to give him self-control as he waited for God to remove Saul from the throne. He did not run rashly ahead of God even though the opportunity presented itself on two occasions (cf. 1 Sam. 24:1ff; 26:6ff).

The pattern that Peter spelled out in his first chapter was acted out in David's life. He put his faith to work, and his faith produced moral excellence, knowledge, and self-control. When we put our faith to work, there is no need for panic, for we know that God has provided all that we need for life and godliness; and there are no surprises, for we believe that God is in control of all things and nothing will ever get out of hand.

"In your self-control, perseverance." Long-distance runners count on the appearance of a "second wind" at some point in their race. It usually comes after the initial store of energy has been depleted and a feeling of exhaustion appears for a moment. The runner knows that the "second wind" will come only if he continues to run even though legs and lungs are urging him to quit. This experience is a parable of the Christian life. Peter promised his readers that when they put their faith to work, the power to persevere would be found in the resources of faith, moral excellence, knowledge, and self-control.

The Hebrews were in danger of losing their perseverance. Life was just too much of a struggle to continue in their faith. See how the author of the Book of Hebrews dealt with their weakness. First, he reminded them of the content of their faith: they believed in a God of holiness (10:30). So he quoted from Isaiah 26:11 and Deuteronomy 32:35f. Next, he reminded them of former days when their faith produced the moral excellence of courage, sympathy, joy, and hope (vv. 32f). Next, he called for confidence and boldness lest in a fit of rashness they throw away their self-control, for, he wrote, "you have need of endurance, so that when you have done the will of God, you may receive what was promised" (v. 36). He followed the pattern outlined by Peter and urged the people to be patient until they received their second wind.

"In your perseverance, godliness." The word "godliness" is a translation of a Greek word that often means piety. It is a reverence for gods as well as parents in classical Greek. But as Arndt and Gingrich point out,[3] in the Greek translation of the Old Testament and in the New Testament, the word is only used of the duty which we owe to God. An endurance produced by faith results in godliness, because trials and difficulties drive us to God. The opposite, "godlessness," with its attendant vices and anarchy, is derived from unbelief when such unbelief is placed in the crucible of trouble.

When Eve named Cain, she was evidently filled with hopes for an early fulfillment of God's promise in the garden. She called him Cain because she had "gotten a manchild with the help of the Lord" (Gen. 4:1). However, she called her second son "Abel" which means "vanity," or "to no purpose," probably because she was becoming more aware of the effects of the curse.

The two boys grew up amid the growing tyranny of the curse. The believing Abel worshiped, bringing an offering of the flock, especially the fat portions. The faithless Cain also worshiped, but there was something about his offering which was unacceptable to God (Heb. 11:4). Cain's problems drove him further from the Lord; he was angered at God's righteous judgment, rejected God's word of admonition, committed murder, and then complained because of his punishment.

Unbelief was producing the works of the flesh in Cain. Trouble is an instrument for good only in the atmosphere of faith. Unbelief may only pretend to produce good. Usually it conduces to evil such as hatred and bitterness toward both God and man.

Perhaps Peter was drawing attention to the difference between the Stoic virtue "apathy," which is produced out of the resources to which a human being is restricted, and the Christian virtue that derives its strength from God even when it is tried for a long time.

"In your godliness, brotherly kindness." There is a form of piety and religiosity that separates people from their neighbors. As a wag once put it, "We can become so heavenly that we are no earthly good." It is quite clear that Peter does not have this in mind. True godliness drives people to brotherly kindness, that is, a love among the members of Christ's body, the church.

The grievous error of mistaking piety for ritual duties to God to the neglect of people was the error committed by the Pharisees. They were meticulous in their duties toward God. Of them Jesus said, "You tithe mint and dill and cummin" (Matt. 23:23). They took the levitical law seriously (Lev.

27:30) that required the Israelite to tithe the seed of the land and the fruit of the tree. Some of the Pharisees thus undertook to tithe whatever they ate or bought or sold, and they were meticulous in this. So exacting were they in these duties (which went well beyond what the law required) that Jesus accused them of neglecting "the weightier provisions of the law: justice, mercy, and faithfulness." We should note in this regard that Jesus also opposed the other extreme of neglecting duties to God in zeal to have compassion on others. He had a balanced view of life: "these [justice, mercy, faithfulness] are things you should have done without neglecting the others [tithes]."

Godliness produces brotherly kindness because our faith teaches us that we belong to other Christians, all of us being united to Christ and to each other in His body. Hence, "the members should have the same care for one another" (1 Cor. 12:25; cf. Gal. 6:10).

But there is another consideration which leads to brotherly kindness. It is a fact of Scripture that we are not able to give to God, for He has no need (Ps. 50:10-13). In fact, the only way we can show our love to God is by showing it to others (Matt. 10:40; 25:31ff).

So the saints must put their faith to work. There is no tension between duties to God and our neighbor, nor is there any way to avoid the social implications of the Gospel. A proper view of godliness leads to brotherly kindness.

Such brotherly kindness will lead to love, for Peter concluded the list by saying, "In your brotherly kindness, love." Probably Peter intended that his readers think of love beyond the Christian community, to the love that Christians should feel toward a neighbor no matter what his beliefs may be.

When we consider that "love" comes at the end of the series, we probably should see it in relation to its predecessors.

— Our *faith* teaches us to love our enemies, to preach the Gospel to the lost, and to be a kingdom of priests to the nations of the earth.

— The *moral excellence* which grows out of faith is, as we suggested above, Christlikeness that entails a compassion like His, a compassion for people in their need.

— The *experiential* knowledge that flows from moral excellence creates a sympathy for people who are not so blessed as we. Did not God require of Israel to treat strangers kindly, "since you yourselves know the feelings of a stranger, for you also were strangers in the land of Egypt" (Ex. 23:9). We cannot forget what we were, so we must always have sympathy for those in a similar situation.

— The *self-control* that is included in that knowledge is based on a fear of passions run rampant. If we desire to control our own sinful emotions, we shall not easily overlook the damage which can be done by the strong feelings of others, and in mercy seek to release them from passion's hold.

— *Perseverance* creates an understanding love for others. Joseph, after a long siege of troubles, could pray for and forgive his brothers. Job evidently had nothing but compassion for his misguided friends, and he interceded for them before God.

— *Godliness*, though it has God as its focus, cannot (as we have seen) ignore His concern for others.

— *Brotherly kindness*, though it is directed toward the saints within the fellowship, must soon overflow to those without, since many of the same motives that produce love for the saints must also produce love for others (Matt. 5:44ff).

During a recent three-months stay in Roorkee, India, I spoke on Second Peter in the chapel services of the Presbyterian Theological Seminary. Sometimes I wondered if my Western style of teaching was understood by our friends in India. Upon returning, however, we received a Christmas card from a student with the appended note that he was still "opening boxes!"

"Faith works," wrote Paul in Galatians 5:6. Peter agreed and showed that a long list of fruit is contained within that faith. The great challenge of the Bible is therefore, "Put your faith to work."

Questions for Chapter 14

1. Study Peter's life to see how faith contained all things necessary for life and godliness. Note that Peter's lapses illustrate this as well as his victories.
2. Show how Peter's faith was really "of the same kind" as that of other saints in Scripture or in your own experiences.
3. Are there other fruit, not mentioned by Peter, that are included within "faith"?

Notes

[1] *Systematic Theology,* Vol. III, p. 93.
[2] *Biblical Doctrines,* p. 483.
[3] *A Greek-English Lexicon of the New Testament*, p. 326.

Chapter 15

The Fruit and God

FAITH PRODUCES LOVE. That is Peter's message. Paul's teaching is to the same effect, but from a slightly different point of view. He wrote, "Faith works through love" (Gal. 5:6). Love is the medium through which faith works, it is the atmosphere in which the fruit grow and abound. As Paul pointed out later in the chapter, hatred destroys (vv. 15, 26). Only through love's agency can the fruit of the Spirit grow.

For the purposes of developing this thought more specifically, let me diagram these relationships that will be discussed at some length in the succeeding chapters.

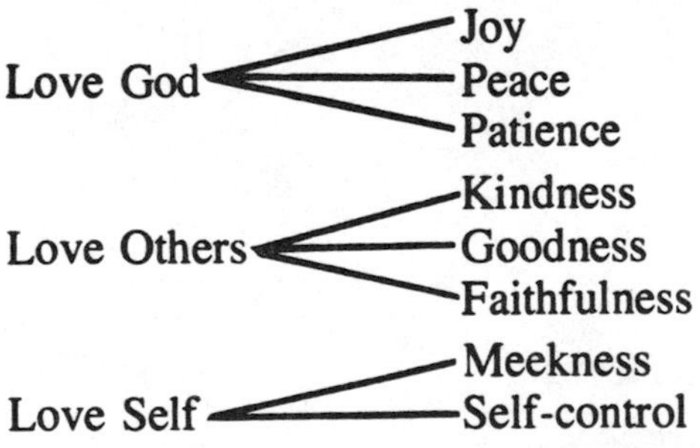

A number of years ago a book appeared with the title *You*

Are What You Eat. The author analyzed various foods as to their caloric content, vitamin supply, and protein and urged his readers to eat well so that they might live well. I should like to rephrase his title to read, "You Are What You Think." The thought is certainly biblical. The Psalmist predicted that idol-worshipers would become like the gods they worshiped (Ps. 115:8). Paul commanded the Romans to "be transformed by the renewing of your mind" (Rom. 12:2). Charles Hodge spoke of it as "that renewing of the mind which produces a transformation of character."[1]

One of the great tasks of a new Christian is to renew his mind regarding God. How else can a person love God with all his heart? When we meditate on God's glorious attributes, when such contemplation leads to love which responds to His, then there is developed a climate in which the fruit of joy, peace, and patience thrive.

Before entering into this discussion, we must consider a few points. First, joy, peace, and patience are, as I have insisted in the earlier part of the book, not traits of character that can be induced by education, home training, or psychological techniques. They are truly created by the Spirit in the personality of the believer at the moment of the new birth. Second, they are therefore beyond the reach of mere human endeavor. Notice how the writers of Scripture speak of them: "joy *inexpressible*" (1 Peter 1:8); "the peace of God, which *surpasses all comprehension*" (Phil. 4:7); "the endurance *of Job*" (James 5:11) [italics mine]. These are not superlatives; they are beyond the superlative! The apostles set before us as normal Christian experience, not the possible, but the impossible. In His blessed sanctifying work the Spirit bestows the fruit and grants the enablement for us to do our part in producing it. On the human side, they are produced in an atmosphere of love toward God, but they are definitely the fruit *of the Spirit*!

Sovereignty

What is it in the character of God which, as we think of

Him, produces joy, peace, and patience? In the first place, the truth of His sovereignty is indispensable to such traits in us. Notice Paul's joy, peace, and patience as his prison ship made its way to Rome (Acts 27). Even though the centurion, the ship's pilot, and captain had rejected his advice (vv. 10f) and had brought the entire ship's company into grave danger, Paul encouraged them with the word, received from an angel, that the sovereign God would preserve them all alive even though the ship would be lost. Note the calm assurance of his words, "for I believe God, that it will turn out exactly as I have been told" (v. 25); "not a hair from the head of any of you shall perish" (v. 34). Despite the danger, Paul demonstrated his inner serenity by offering a prayer of thanksgiving for food, then eating in view of them all.

Later Paul's faith in God's sovereign promise that he would surely reach Rome (27:24) was sorely tested on the island of Malta (28:1ff). There he was bitten by a snake, known to the islanders to be poisonous. Paul simply shook off the snake and was obviously unharmed. Luke recorded no panic on Paul's part, only the amazement of the islanders.

Paul expressed his faith in God's sovereignty in Ephesians 1:11: "Also we have obtained an inheritance, having been predestined according to His purpose who works all things after the counsel of His will." In this verse Paul was describing the inheritance of Jewish Christians. "As the Israelites of old obtained an inheritance in the promised land, so those in Christ become partakers of that heavenly inheritance which he has secured for them."[2] Now this inheritance was certain, because God works *all things* according to that plan which has its origin in *His* will. It was not a chance event, else there would be no certainty. Neither did it depend on human effort, or they could never be sure of it. Their inheritance depended solely on God's will, and that made it gloriously certain.

Now it is just the "all things" that brought comfort and joy to Paul. Since God was in control, there was no place in a Christian consciousness for sorrow, fretting, and impatience.

This verse has been a source of great comfort to me ever since the Holy Spirit (as I sincerely believe) brought it to my attention in a time of crisis. Back in 1942 our small family of three was involved in an automobile accident. Our small baby was thrown to the floor of the car, his head cut; my wife suffered bruises; my head smashed through the windshield and I was momentarily unconscious. As I came to, I could not see and could only hear the moans of my wife and the cries of our baby. Panic such as I had never known it in my life swept over me. The situation seemed desperate, since we were in a lightly traveled area of St. Louis County. Almost instantly, however, the situation changed dramatically as the words of Ephesians 1:11 came to mind: "Who works all things after the counsel of His will." In a manner I cannot explain, hopelessness changed to peace, panic gave way to deliberation. Although it was by no means clear how we would find help, there was unmistakable joy, peace, and patience all through the wait for help, a week's siege in the hospital, and many uncertainties along the way. When we put our faith to work and believe that God is all He says He is, then the fruit of the Spirit appear.

As we reflect on God's sovereignty, we can say, "He could have prevented this. Since He did not, He must have willed it, and so it is all right."

Wisdom

God's wisdom, as we contemplate it, also gives us joy, peace, and patience. God's wise control over history means that nothing comes into the life of a child of God as an afterthought, a blunder, an unforeseen circumstance, or a mistake. Moreover, since God's wisdom is so far superior to ours, His actions may on first glance seem very strange indeed. We must be prepared for strange and seemingly senseless circumstances because God's judgments are unsearchable and His ways are unfathomable (Rom. 11:33).

A set of such strange circumstances befell Saul in First Samuel 9. He did not know it, but God had planned to place him on Israel's throne in response to the people's rash prayer. All Saul knew was that his father Kish told him the family donkeys were lost. Now the loss of such animals on a Benjamite farm was the same as your car's being lost, or your vacuum cleaner's not operating on the day you expect important guests — it was a minor tragedy. Saul was told to look for them. He and a servant wandered over the area of Benjamin and Judah, but they were disappointed in their search. Note the words of v. 4: " . . . they did not find them . . . they were not there . . . they did not find them." They had failed! Discouragement set in: "Come, and let us return, lest my father cease to be concerned about the donkeys and become anxious for us" (v. 5).

If young Saul gave any thought to God's hand in all this, he could have made out an impressive case that there was no God, or He didn't care, or He hated Saul, or He was helpless to do him any good. Look at the facts: loss, disappointment, discouragement, failure! Is this a normal life for a worshiper of God? Well, it certainly is not unusual, as many saints can testify.

In the sequel Saul viewed things differently. What had seemed failure and inconvenience were simply links in a chain of wisely forged circumstances. Samuel the prophet was to anoint the new king, and it was necessary to bring Samuel and Saul together. The means God had chosen were loss, disappointment, discouragement, failure. Could He have chosen a happier set of circumstances? Of course He could have, but He chose not to, and we must leave it there. As things stand, God used these means to make Saul king of Israel (1 Sam. 10:1ff), and in the meantime someone else had found the donkeys!

The Oxford English Dictionary[3] defines "wisdom" as "soundness of judgment in the choice of means and ends." When a Christian ascribes wisdom to God, this is certainly one facet which belongs to Him supremely. When we put our faith in God to work, we experience joy, peace, and patience, since we are trusting in a God who is wholly wise.

Righteousness

God's righteousness, as we meditate on it, is also an

occasion for joy, peace, and patience. To some people, on a superficial glance, God's righteousness is a terrifying thing; but to the saints it can be a source of profound comfort. Take Abraham, as an example (Gen. 18 and 19). God told him that He would destroy Sodom and Gomorrah, cities of the Jordan plain. Lot, Abraham's nephew, had settled there (14:10ff), and Abraham feared for the lives of Lot and his family. Abraham's prayer of intercession is a beautiful incident in an otherwise sordid story of compromise and depravity. It is a prayer in which Abraham seems to rise higher and higher in urgency and boldness. His concern is for the righteous. Evidently Abraham knew of Lot's commitment to God, even though our reading of the history won't make that obvious (yet cf. 2 Peter 2:7).

The basis of Abraham's prayer for the righteous was the conviction that God is righteous. "Far be it from Thee to do such a thing, to slay the righteous with the wicked, so that the righteous and the wicked are treated alike. Far be it from Thee! Shall not the Judge of all the earth deal justly?" (Gen. 18:25). Abraham's confidence in prayer, accompanied with appropriate humility and awareness of the majesty of God (18:27, 30, 32), had its basis in God's righteousness, and he clung to that basis to the end of that prayer.[4]

In what follows we see that Abraham's belief of God's righteousness was confirmed, and that in a very striking way. In chapter 19, as Lot's family delayed their flight from Sodom, the angel urged them on by saying, "Hurry, escape there [to Zoar], for I cannot do anything until you arrive there." Note, "I cannot do anything." Again, I quote from Calvin:

> And let us especially remember, that his power is connected by a sacred bond with his grace, and with faith in his promises. Hence it may be truly and properly said, that he can do nothing but what he wills and promises. This is a true and profitable doctrine.[5]

I would like to pay tribute to a very godly young woman, now in glory, whose life bore testimony to her conviction of the righteousness of God. At her wedding, the congregation sang, "Whate'er my God ordains is right." The theme of that song is God's righteous provision for His own children. Some years later, as she was watching her little boy grow, her nurse's instinct told her that something was wrong with him. A doctor's preliminary diagnosis was that the child, about a year old, might be physically retarded and might even be blind. At the next prayer meeting of our church, she came with her family and was holding her son on her lap when the pastor asked if someone had a favorite hymn for us to sing. At once she asked for "Whate'er my God ordains is right," and though it was difficult for most of us to do, we sang it with her as a demonstration of her faith:

> Whate'er my God ordains is right: Holy his will abideth;
> I will be still whate'er he doth, And follow where he guideth:
> He is my God; Though dark my road, He holds me that I shall not fall:
> Wherefore to him I leave it all.
>
> Whate'er my God ordains is right: He never will deceive me;
> He leads me by the proper path; I know he will not leave me:
> I take, content, What he hath sent; His hand can turn my griefs away,
> And patiently I wait his day.
>
> Whate'er my God ordains is right: Though now this cup, in drinking,
> May bitter seem to my faint heart, I take it, all unshrinking:
> My God is true; Each morn anew Sweet comfort yet shall fill my heart,
> And pain and sorrow shall depart.
>
> Whate'er my God ordains is right: Here shall my stand be taken;
> Though sorrow, need, or death be mine, Yet am I not forsaken;
> My Father's care Is round me there; He holds me that I shall not fall:
> And so to him I leave it all.

Just recently we were called upon to sing that song again as a congregation — at her funeral. With no forewarning, she collapsed one morning and was pronounced dead on arrival at the hospital. She was carrying her third child at the time, and she left her husband and two small children without a wife and mother. As we sang that hymn again, it was with a greater sense of God's righteousness than ever before, because she had lived so calmly and sweetly in the assurance of His sovereign justice.

It is one thing to sing such a song when nothing is wrong. It is another to sing it and find joy, peace, and patience when everything as far as you can see seems so unfair and not right. No one who knew Becky Emerson Ferguson could doubt that her resources for the fruit of the Spirit were deep in the righteousness of God.

The fruit of the Spirit often appears when it is least expected. It is for this reason that its God-given character is most important to stress. In my younger days I came to know of Dr. Howard A. Kelly of the faculty of medicine at Johns Hopkins Medical School in Baltimore. A surgeon of world renown, Dr. Kelly was one of the "big four" who gave Johns Hopkins its reputation. He was also a fearless Christian who spoke and wrote in defense of the faith in the days when denial of the virgin birth of Jesus was front-page copy.

However, Dr. Kelly witnessed for Christ in other ways. "Dr. Kelly was very fond of flowers, and in his buttonhole he daily wore a pink rose, kept fresh by inserting its stem into a small water-filled vial pinned to the underside of the coat lapel. The rose, too, afforded an opening for a discussion of his faith. When its freshness and beauty were remarked, he would say, 'This is a Christian rose (turning over the lapel to reveal the stem in water), with hidden sources of grace and life.' "[6]

"Hidden sources of grace and life." Surely one of those sources is the faith which cries out, "Shall not the Judge of all the earth deal justly?"

Love

God's love, when we think of it, will bring us to joy, peace, and patience. Since His love for His saints characterizes all that He does for them, what happens must be understood as flowing from His love (cf. Heb. 12:5, 6). Because God has determined that the message of His love be disseminated throughout the world, the events of our lives should be understood as contributing to the Great Commission. It was this conviction that led Paul to write Philippians, often called "the epistle of joy." It is all the more remarkable that he experienced this joy, because he was in prison, doubtless chained to a Roman soldier. "He glories in his chains more than a king in his diadem" (Theodoret).[7]

His joy is yet more significant, since no legitimate charge had been placed against Paul. Yet he did not complain. To the contrary he wrote: "Now I want you to know, brethren, that my circumstances have turned out for the greater progress of the Gospel" (1:12). Not only were Christians outside of prison given courage to preach, but the praetorian guard knew of Paul's imprisonment for the sake of Christ.

There isn't much justice in the world today, but God may well be using instances of gross unfairness to the saints as vehicles for spreading His Gospel. The saints, if they are true to their sainthood, won't frequent the jails of our country. But if a witness is to reach jailers and inmates, some Christians may have to suffer unjustly so that they can carry the message there.

One final remark. A person might conclude from what has been said that the Christian life is one of passivity only, i.e., all we do is meekly acquiesce in the outworkings of God's providence. But obviously Abraham did not. Nor did Kish simply wring his hands at the loss of the donkeys. The Christian life promotes a delicate balance between a joyful acceptance of God's plan, and a determination to see that His revealed will is brought to fulfillment here on the earth.

Questions for Chapter 15

1. Does our love for God also have a part in producing the other fruit: kindness, goodness, faithfulness, meekness, and self-control? If you think so, show how.
2. I have stressed four attributes of God: sovereignty, wis-

dom, righteousness, and love in the production of the fruit. Think of other attributes and relate them to joy, peace, and patience.

3. When you are faced with a problem, how do you decide whether to accept it as from God, or to seek to change it? For example, if you had been in Abraham's shoes, would you have interceded for Sodom?

Notes

[1] *Commentary on the Epistle to the Romans*, p. 394.

[2] C. Hodge, *Commentary on the Epistle to the Ephesians*, p. 56.

[3] *The Compact Edition of the Oxford English Dictionary*, Vol. II, p. 3794.

[4] Calvin's words at this point are most helpful: "For although he wonders how God should think of destroying Sodom, in which he was persuaded there was a number of good men; he yet retains this principle, that it was impossible for God, who is the Judge of the world, and by nature loves equity, yea, whose will is the law of justice and rectitude, should in the least degree swerve from righteousness. He desires, however, to be relieved from this difficulty with which he is perplexed. So, whenever different temptations contend within our minds, and some appearance of contradiction presents itself in the works of God, only let our persuasion of His justice remain fixed, and we shall be permitted to pour into His bosom the difficulties which torment us, in order that He may loosen the knots which we cannot untie. Paul seems to have taken from this place the answer with which he represses the blasphemy of those who charge God with unrighteousness. 'Is God unrighteous? Far from it, for how should there be unrighteousness with Him who judges the world?' (Rom. 3:5, 6). This method of appeal would not always avail among earthly judges; who are sometimes deceived by error, or perverted by favour, or inflamed with hatred, or corrupted by gifts, or misled by other means, to acts of injustice. But since God, to whom it naturally belongs to judge the world, is liable to none of these evils, it follows, that He can no more be drawn aside from equity, than he can deny himself to be God" (*Commentaries on the Book of Genesis*, Vol. I, p. 489).

[5] *Ibid.*, p. 511.

[6] Audrey W. Davis, *Dr. Kelly of Hopkins* (The Johns Hopkins Press, Baltimore), p. 173f.

[7] Quoted by Charles Hodge, *Commentary on the Epistle to the Ephesians*, p. 198.

Chapter 16

The Fruit and Others

WHEN WE PUT OUR FAITH in God to work, we respond to the message of His love by a love of our own, and in the atmosphere produced by that love there develops within us the fruit of joy, peace, and patience. Theoretically such a love on our part should be a natural and readily produced response. God is such a wonderful and adorable Being — how can we but love Him? But of course we know that, practically, it is not so. Sin being what it is, this "great and foremost commandment" (Matt. 22:38) is impossible to keep apart from grace.

By contrast, the second great commandment should be much more difficult. What is there in sinful humanity that commands unqualified respect, let alone love? Who can love people who live in the manner described in Appendix A, page 179? Of course we may tone down our conception of love to a point where it becomes mere tolerance of others — so long as they do not interfere in our lives! But God will not settle for mere tolerance of others on our part. He not only commands love, but defines it for us (cf. chapter 5) and makes quite explicit that when we put our faith to work, we shall develop a love for others that shows itself as kindness, goodness, and faithfulness.

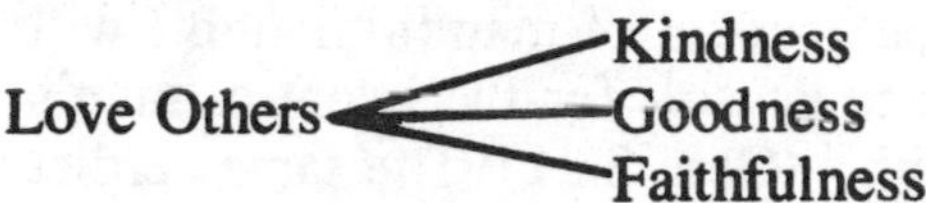

But once again we must examine our faith so that we may put it to work. What is there in our faith that makes it possible, and even inevitable, that we shall love our neighbor as we love ourselves? I suggest that there are at least three important truths: the teachings regarding the image of God in man; those regarding the sovereignty of God in our lives; and the command to treat another as if he were Jesus.

The Image of God

When the flood was over and the waters had receded, and the covenant was being renewed with Noah as a new head of the race, God gave Noah some commandments. One of them had to do with murder and its punishment: "Whoever sheds man's blood, by man his blood shall be shed, for in the image of God He made man" (Gen. 9:6). This commandment must be seen in its context. God had just given the race an enlarged diet—meat was now permitted, providing only its blood was excluded. It was not a sin to take an animal's life. No penalty was laid down for a slayer of animals.

But a severe penalty would be required of the slayer of a human being — his life must be taken to indicate the enormity of his crime. But what's the difference between a man and a beast? Modern developmental evolutionary theory cannot give us an answer. But God made it clear to Noah— "in the image of God He made man." Any human being— no matter how deep into sin he may have fallen — has a dignity and a value because he is the image of God.

The Flood, you see, had not changed the race's involvement in sin. Before the deluge "the Lord saw that the wickedness of man was great on the earth, and that every intent of the thoughts of his heart was only evil continually" (Gen. 6:5). After the waters subsided and only eight human beings remained — saved from destruction because Noah had found grace in God's sight — God said, "I will never again curse the ground on account of man [although I will have many provocations to do so], for the intent of man's heart is evil from his youth" (Gen. 8:21). The same verdict was passed both before and after the flood. The race continued in sin, but also it continued as God's image — marred no doubt and frequently distorted beyond recognition; but nevertheless the image remained as something sacred, and to destroy it was a crime worthy of death.

In the New Testament, James said very much the same thing: In chapter 3 of his epistle, he wrote about the way people abuse one another by their tongues. Tongues are such little things, yet can do a world of damage. In the context of saying all this, James wrote of the paradox of blessing God with our tongue and cursing people with the same tongue. The anomaly lies in the fact that the people we curse "have been made in the likeness of God" (3:9). Thus, "from the same mouth come forth both blessing and cursing" of the same image.

If we look on others, not because of what they are in themselves, but because of whose image they bear, they will provoke us to kindness, goodness, and faithfulness. This is not psychological role-playing, or a philosophical attitude of "as if," but appreciation of the reality which our faith leads us to accept as true of our neighbor.

The Sovereignty of God

In the last chapter we saw how joy, peace, and patience grow within us as we put to work our faith in God's sovereignty. This same doctrine will lead us to kindness, goodness, and faithfulness toward others when we consider that what our neighbor might plan for our hurt, God has planned for good.

I have had occasion to remark on the Christlikeness of Joseph, who treated his brothers so well after they had done him so much evil. Notice his kindness: "I will also provide for you . . . lest you and your household and all that you have be impoverished'' (Gen. 45:11); his goodness and generosity: ''Joseph settled his father and his brothers, and gave them a possession in the land of Egypt, in the best of the land'' (47:11); his faithfulness: after their father Jacob died, the brothers feared that Joseph would go back on his word and retaliate, but instead ''he comforted them and spoke kindly to them'' (50:21), remembering his earlier words of promise.

It is perfectly clear that the fruit of the Spirit grew as Joseph contemplated God's sovereignty. It is equally clear that a similar result will be found in us when we follow his example.

> . . . whenever the Lord interposes to prevent the evil of those who desire to injure us, and not that only, but turns even their wicked designs to our good; he subdues, by this method, our carnal affections, and renders us more just and placable. Thus we see that Joseph was a skillful interpreter of the providence of God, when he borrowed from it an argument for granting forgiveness to his brethren. The magnitude of the crime committed against him might so have incensed him as to cause him to burn with the desire of revenge: but when he reflects that their wickedness had been overruled by the wonderful and unwonted goodness of God, forgetting the injury received, he kindly embraces the men whose dishonor God had covered with his grace. And true charity is ingenious in hiding the faults of brethren, and therefore she freely applies to this use anything which may tend to appease anger, and to set enmities at rest.[1]

Treating Others as We Would Jesus

In the gospel of Matthew Jesus spoke of a third principle that will help us to love other people, no matter how unlovable they may be: ''Truly I say to you, to the extent that you did it to one of these brothers of Mine, even the least of them, you did it to Me'' (25:40). This is perhaps an extension of Proverbs 19:17: ''He who is gracious to a poor man lends to the Lord, and He will repay him for his good deed.''

This principle is vividly and beautifully illustrated in James Russell Lowell's *The Vision of Sir Launfal*. The poem begins in the early summer with a young knight setting forth on a powerful steed to search for the Holy Grail. He crossed the moat which surrounded the castle, full of zeal and determination. So intent on the importance of his goal was he that the leper crouching by the castle's gate only filled him with loathing:

> The sunshine went out of his soul with a thrill,
> The flesh 'neath his armor 'gan shrink and crawl,
> And midway its leap his heart stood still
> Like a frozen waterfall;
> For this man, so foul and bent of stature,
> Rasped harshly against his dainty nature,
> And seemed the one blot on the summer morn, —
> So he tossed him a piece of gold in scorn.[2]

Then, off into the world in search of the Holy Grail!

The poem ends as a very discouraged and disillusioned knight, now mature in years, limped castleward on his broken charger. He had gone over the whole world, but had not found his treasure. Strangely enough, the beggar was still at the gate of the castle's grounds. But now the knight had time for him; he dismounted and proceeded to share with the beggar the single crust of bread left in his bag. He prayed,

> 'Mild Mary's Son, acknowledge me;
> Behold, through him, I give to thee!'

Then something happened:

> As Sir Launfal mused with a downcast face,
> A light shone round about the place;
> The leper no longer crouched at his side,
> But stood before him glorified. . . .
> And the voice that was calmer than silence said,
> 'Lo, it is I, be not afraid!
> In many climes without avail,
> Thou hast spent thy life for the Holy Grail;
> Behold it is here, — this cup which thou
> Didst fill at the streamlet for me but now; . . .[3]

Lowell's thought — that Jesus Christ often appears in unlikely disguises: ugly and repugnant; and that He is not afar off but often right in our pathway — accords with Scripture. We can accept the repulsiveness of other people and show them gentleness, goodness, and faithfulness when we recall the promise, "To the extent that you did it to one of these brothers of Mine, even the least of them, you did it to Me."

This truth has implications for evangelistic service of all kinds and in different places. We take the Gospel to the unrighteous, to sinners, the ungodly. We are never told that sinners are attractive, or that they will treat us well. The experience of the apostle Paul in Acts 16 may be instructive. In a vision a man of Macedonia appealed to him to come to northern Greece to "help us." Immediately Paul and his companions set out for Philippi, one of the chief cities of the district. His first convert was Lydia. But soon Paul and the others were haled before the authorities and beaten with rods and imprisoned, their feet fastened in stocks. (vv. 22ff). After the jailer was converted, the magistrates begged Paul to leave the city. Exhorting the infant church (v. 40), they did just that.

On balance one would not say that Macedonians as a whole were particularly eager to have Paul in their city. Was the vision a false one?

In Thessalonica (17:1), after a larger number believed, the apostolic group was mobbed, and peace did not come until Jason posted a bond that secured Paul's person. Again Paul and Silas were sent away, this time by their converts, and they went to Berea. Again, some converts; but again, agitation and "perils of the Gentiles" (2 Cor. 11:26). Silas and Timothy could stay, but Paul left for the seacoast beyond the bounds of Macedonia. Was Paul really wanted in Macedonia?

The point is, the man of Macedonia in Paul's vision represented the believers *after* they had been called by the Spirit to Jesus (16:14). They wanted Paul and his message *after* they realized their peril and the safety promised them in the Gospel. The vision anticipated changed lives, and Paul responded to the people, not as they were, but as they would be once the Gospel had been preached to them.

Similarly today, the call to evangelistic service of any sort is not based on the attractiveness of people as they now are, but on the anticipated attractiveness when they are renewed by the Spirit of God.

The choice is ours. We may harbor "enmities, strife, jealousy, outbursts of anger . . . and such like" within our souls because of the evil actions of others — and the bitterness of spirit will destroy us, not them! Or we may show gentleness, goodness, and faithfulness to even the worst — and the exhilaration of spirit will serve to preserve us and them.

Questions for Chapter 16

1. What characteristics in people today show that they are still God's image? How is this doctrine different from the "spark of divinity" which liberals used to talk about?
2. Why does God in His providence permit so much evil in the world? in the church? In this connection, study Psalm 76:10.
3. In Hebrews 13:2 we are commanded to entertain strangers. How far should we go in seeking to obey this command?
4. What is the difference between humanistic philanthropy and a biblical love of neighbors?

Notes

[1] J. Calvin, *Commentaries on the Book of Genesis*, Vol. II, p. 380.

[2] *The Vision of Sir Launfal*, Part First.

[3] Part Second.

Chapter 17

The Fruit and Ourselves

LOVE IS A many-faceted thing. Our love to God is devotion, confidence, and sheer joy. Our love for others is a concern for what is best for them. Our love for ourselves entails an acceptance of what God in His Word has said about us.

Most of us are afraid of self-love, of self-esteem. We feel it is inconsistent with what the Bible says about our sinfulness and depravity. Isn't it better to hate ourselves, deny ourselves, or crucify ourselves, than to love ourselves? It is true: in some contexts we are to hate ourselves (Luke 14:26); deny ourselves (Matt. 16:24); and crucify ourselves (Gal. 6:14). If it is a question of human merit offered to God as a ground for our justification, we can only hate ourselves. When it is a matter of human desire in defiance to the law of God, we can only deny ourselves.

However, the same Scriptures that speak of these things also call us "saints" (1 Cor. 1:2) and "able ministers" (2 Cor. 3:6, KJV); they describe us as "full of goodness, filled with all knowledge, and able also to admonish one another" (Rom. 15:14). We can no more reject the one than the other description of us.

As an example of how far we have gone to adopt the customs of the Roman Catholics, I frequently ask congregations their reaction to calling one of their number "Saint Charles" or "Saint Raymond." There is usually a titter throughout the audience, and most people react with grins of amusement. The implication is that they *know* these people; *they* couldn't be called saints! But it is Romanist thinking that has elevated only a certain group of people to sainthood; it is biblical thinking to call any child of God a saint. We should be free to call ourselves by biblically sanctioned titles, and when we do that we are speaking of ourselves in the highest of terms. But this is just what God does.

There is a scriptural basis for self-love, and Jesus was not just speaking rhetorically when He commanded us to love our neighbors as we love ourselves. We cannot deny that God has done great things for us and in us. I have already referred to Dr. Buswell's remark based on Ephesians 1:18 — "He has made you worth-while" (p. 105).

So again, we must put our faith to work. We must believe what God has said about us, accept ourselves for what we are, and demonstrate a proper and balanced concern for what is best for us. When we do this, we will develop the fruit of the Spirit of meekness and self-control.

Faith → Love Self → Meekness
Faith → Love Self → Self-control

What does our faith teach us about ourselves? In the life of David we may learn a proper evaluation of ourselves because his faults and his virtues are set before us with startling clarity.

Propensity to Sin

First, his faults teach us that we all have inherited a basic propensity to sin. Who would have thought that the "sweet singer of Israel," "the man after God's own heart," could have been guilty of adultery, murder, deceit, and judicial rashness? It all happened at a high point in David's life (2 Sam. 11:1ff). He had glowing successes as king, general, and religious reformer. But despite the security these things might have brought him, he fell quickly. Although the adultery alone was premeditated, the murder and deceit soon followed under the pressure of a guilty conscience and a desire to cover up. Then when he was faced by Nathan with an imaginary situation of covetousness, he rashly condemned the supposed culprit to death — a penalty far in excess of the law's demands — and did so without the testimony of the required two witnesses.

The picture is not a happy one, but it is not intended to be. It is a revelation of David's propensity to sin, but of ours also. Anyone who loves himself will seek to understand his peril in this matter, will seek for Spirit-guided self-control, and will never think more highly of himself than he ought to think. Moreover, he will not willingly allow himself to be put in places where temptation will cause this propensity to rear its ugly head. This is true meekness and self-control, or at least one important aspect of it.

Accepting Ourselves

But David had virtues as well, and a study of them will indicate to us truly biblical meekness. Following Nathan's rebuke (2 Sam. 12:1ff), the child born to Bathsheba and David became very sick, just as the prophet had predicted (v. 14). David prayed fervently until he realized that the answer to his prayer was No. Instead of reproaching God, he accepted the news calmly, bathed, changed his clothes, worshiped in the house of the Lord, and then ate for the first time in a week.

In a number of ways the account indicates David's meekness and self-control. First, he knew who he was (a creature and a sinner), and he knew who God was (the Creator and righteous Judge). Meekness is "accepting ourselves as we really are" (cf. pp. 128f), and David's acquiescence in God's refusal to answer his prayer was based on his understanding of the real situation existing between God and himself. Self-control entails the choice of "the best of all goals, God's glory, and the power to make progress towards it" (cf. p. 138) and David chose God's will over his own, despite the fact that his heart was breaking.

Second, David probably surprised some people when he went to the house of God to worship. Should a known adulterer, a liar, and murderer be seen in the house of God, even if he is king? Certainly God had disciplined his child, not in the way outlined in the Mosaic law, but in accordance with His own desires. Even so, some might have questioned the propriety of David's appearing at worship so soon after his sin had been revealed. But David had solid grounds for doing this. Nathan had said, as God's prophet, "The Lord also has put away your sin" (v. 13). Meekness is accepting what God's word says about us, even when it counters the judgment of other people. It is a true self-love, accepting ourselves to be just what God says we are.

Third, David realized that, contrary to a brewery's slogan that "We only go around once," what we may not have in this life may yet be ours in the life to come. The child was dead, but the separation was only temporary: "I shall go to him" (v. 23). Too often we are tempted to lose our self-control because the things of this life loom too large on our horizon. The consciousness of a future life (however vague it may have been at David's time) kept David from rash rebellion and arrogance against the Lord. Here again he put his faith to work and accepted his place in God's providence, and the Spirit's fruit became evident.

We should note that our faith does not encourage a life of passivity. To accept God's providence meekly on one occasion is not to be confused with continuous sinful indolence. Nor must we confuse God's providence with fatalism, or meekness with indifference and apathy. We are speaking of a meekness which is courage to be what God has called us to be, and that frequently entails much aggressiveness and activity (Cf. p.128).

Many people today act as if their gift is "occupying a pew." Of course there is no such gift, and nothing said above about meekness should encourage inactivity. The New Testament tells us that each of us has a gift, and meekness means that we recognize that we do, and that we exercise it with every power within us.

Temples of God

The New Testament also teaches that meekness and self-control thrive in an atmosphere of self-love when we realize. the great value which it attaches to our bodies as the temples of God (1 Cor. 3:17; 6:19). His presence bestows a dignity on our flesh of which other religions are ignorant. Therefore we love and cherish our bodies as holy instruments dedicated to God's service. From this fact comes a compulsion to meekness and self-control lest the body be abused and the temple desecrated.

What does it mean to be a "temple of God"? Surely the reference is to the Old Testament temple. Study the chapters in which the temple is described: its planning, the gathering of valuable materials, the elaborate care taken in its construction (1 Kings 5-7; 1 Chron. 28, 29; 2 Chron. 2-5). Note the display of glory as the temple was consecrated (1 Kings 8:11; 2 Chron. 5:14). Note also the encomiums heaped on the city and its temple by the inhabitants of the land (Ps. 48; 50:2). The temple was especially dear to the heart of God, and held in the highest esteem by the people (Ps. 87).

The temple was resplendent because it was the house of God. It typified the incarnation of Jesus Christ (John 2:19ff). But as we have seen, it is a picture of an individual as that person is a habitation of the Spirit.

Did God have a greater concern for His house of stone than He does for His houses of flesh? Was the temple on Zion which was soon to be destroyed of greater value than the humblest believer who will endure forever? What a sobering thought it is that God has made us His dwelling-places! What glory is ours, and what self-control we should exert, to maintain and preserve the glory of God's temples on earth!

SELF-CONTROL IS FREEDOM

A great hindrance to biblical fruit is the contemporary definition of freedom as "the absence of restraint, commandment, or control." It is the opposite of the biblical truth that a disciplined life is real freedom. Much of the false idea of freedom comes from the equally false view that education can produce freedom. Education, so the idea goes, gives us the knowledge of ourselves and of our environment so that we are freed from superstition and thus liberated to control ourselves and our environment in the light of the best scientific and cultural knowledge of the day. Often even the Bible is quoted on the side of this point of view: "You shall know the truth, and the truth shall make you free." This quotation is found on one of the buildings on the campus of Johns Hopkins University in Baltimore.

Dr. Howard A. Kelly, whom I mentioned in chapters 5 and 15, called attention to this misquotation. In a tract entitled, "Kai" (the Greek word for *and*), Dr. Kelly pointed out that John 8:32 really begins with *and*, a word that usually does not appear at the beginning of a sentence. The complete sentence begins in the preceding verse: "Then Jesus said to those Jews which believed on Him, If you continue in My word, then you are My disciples indeed; And you shall know the truth, and the truth shall make you free."

Dr. Kelly's point in the tract was that to omit the *and* and the words of the previous verse is really to misquote. The quotation in its shortened form was the opposite of what Jesus intended, and Jesus' words cannot be used to sanction modern humanist education.

Actually Jesus was calling for biblical self-control as the very gateway to freedom. But such self-control depends on a biblical view of our *selves* as worthy of the best of care and nurture. True Christian freedom is illustrated in Paul's behavior before the high priest (cf. pp. 138f).

Questions for Chapter 17

1. How can we maintain a proper balance between self-reproach ("for such a worm as I") and self-esteem ("Bold shall I stand in that great day")?
2. Think of other biblical illustrations of our "propensity to sin." Why does the Bible tell such stories about God's people? Wouldn't it have been better to suppress these tales?
3. What biblical teachings form a foundation for proper self-love? List as many as you can.
4. What is the difference between "self-control" and "apathy"? How can we have the one and reject the other?

Epilogue

THROUGHOUT THESE STUDIES I have emphasized two things which seem to require repeating as we draw to a close: *the fruit is one;* and *the mere reading about them will not produce them.*

The fruit is one. Paul speaks of fruit, not fruits. We should not think of these character traits as isolated from each other. As we noted on p. 16 faith works through love to produce a many-sided Christian character. To have any of the traits in a truly Christian sense is to have them all.

This will become clearer when we recall that to speak of the fruit is just another way of describing the character of Jesus of Nazareth. As we are being conformed to His image, the fruit in its manifold character is appearing in us.

But for us men, sinners that we are, to be like Jesus Christ is not an easy matter. There is no pat formula. We do not regard the Bible as a cookbook, a "how-to" manual which gives us instructions in righteous living. Paul tells us (in 2 Cor. 3:18) that in the true reading of the Scriptures we see "as in a mirror" Jesus and His glory, and in seeing Him we are changed from glory to glory. There is some sort of mysterious chemistry of the Spirit by which our contemplation of the Scripture produces a change in our character so that we become more like Him.

But James, quite characteristically, reminds us that we may look in the Scriptures and then walk away forgetting what we have heard and seen (1:23f). For both Paul and James the Bible is a book of power and there is no other volume like it in all the world, and the proper reading of the

Bible involves a learning experience different from any other type of education. The true reading of the Scriptures involves the response of faith to the all-powerful Word of God — we respond to God as Creator, Judge, Redeemer. Now this response is not to be limited to one's "quiet time"; it is *a response of the whole man for the whole of life*.

Education in the Scriptural sense entails the response of faith, and faith's response is obedience, and it is in the "exercise" (Heb. 12:11) of faith that the fruit really appears. Without exercise there is no education, and without the exercise of living obedience there is no fruit of the Spirit, no Christlikeness. True, we have been re-created in the image of the loving God, but in life we learn love by loving. For this reason we should see the fruit not only as gracious provision, but also as sovereign demands.

Appendix A

The following catalogs of weeds complement the listing of Galatians 5 (see chapter 4).

Matt. 15:19ff	Rom. 1:29-32	Rom. 13:13	1 Cor. 5:10	2 Cor. 12:20	1 Tim 1:9ff
evil thoughts	covetousness	revelling	fornicators	strife	lawless
murders	maliciousness	drunkenness	covetous	jealousy	unruly
adulteries	envy	immorality	extortioners	wraths	ungodly
fornications	murder	debauchery	idolaters	factions	sinners
thefts	strife	strife	reviler	backbitings	unholy
false witness	deceit	jealousy	drunkard	whisperings	profane
railings	malignity			gossip	patricides
	whispers			disorders	matricides
	backbiters				murderers
	hateful to God				fornicators
	insolent				homosexuals
	haughty				kidnapers
	boastful				liars
	inventors of evil things				false swearers
	disobedient to parents				
	without understanding				
	covenant-breakers				
	without natural affection				
	unmerciful				

Appendix B

A list of suggestions for further study. The list might be much longer. The author will appreciate further suggestions from readers. Obviously, inclusion in this list does not constitute endorsement of book or author.

Personal Holiness

Bolton, Samuel. *The True Bonds of Christian Freedom*. Banner of Truth Trust.

Bonar, H. *God's Way of Holiness*. Moody Press. n.d. A brief but penetrating discussion of several aspects of sanctification.

Buswell, J. O. *Ten Reasons Why a Christian Should Not Live a Wicked Life*. Moody Press. 1959. An exegetical study of Romans 6-8, with a view of Romans 7 quite different from Bonar's and Murray's.

Calvin, John. *Golden Booklet of the True Christian Life*. Baker. 1955. The section on sanctification from his *Institutes*.

Murray, J. *Principles of Conduct*. Wm. B. Eerdmans Publishing Co. 1957. The theory of Christian living. The chapter on "dynamic" is especially helpful.

Ridenour, F. *I'm a Good Man, But*. Regal. Probably most useful with children. Uses Peanuts cartoons to illustrate key points.

Ryle, J. C. *Holiness*. James Clarke. A collection of papers written by one of the more recent "Puritans." 1956.

Social Obligations

Edersheim, A. *Sketches of Jewish Social Life in the Days of Christ*. Wm. B. Eerdmans Publishing Co. 1950. Written during the last century, but throws light on many customs mentioned in the New Testament.

Henry, C. *Aspects of Christian Social Ethics*. Wm. B. Eerdmans Publishing Co., Grand Rapids. 1964.

Hunt, G. *Listen to Me*. IV Press. 1969. Eight university students expose their thinking and attitudes about the world, religion, etc.

Lloyd-Jones, D. M. *Studies in the Sermon on the Mount*. Wm. B. Eerdmans Publishing Co. 1959. Many applications of Jesus' teachings to modern problems.

Oehler, G. *Theology of the Old Testament*. Funk and Wagnalls.

1883. A standard, though old, study in the development of doctrine and practices in the Old Testament.

Richards, L. O. *How Do I Fit In*? Moody Press. Guidelines for interpersonal contacts.

ed. Runner, H. E. *The Bible and the Life of the Christian*. Groen van Prinsterer Society. Calvin College. Grand Rapids. n.d.

Schaeffer, F. *Pollution and the Death of Man*. Tyndale Press. 1970.

Skinner, T. *Words of Revolution*. Zondervan Publishing House. 1970.

Van Riessen, H. *The Society of the Future*. Presbyterian and Reformed Publishing Co. 1952.

Wight, F. H. *Manners and Customs of Bible Lands*. Moody Press. 1953.

Church

Bannerman, D. D. *The Scripture Doctrine of the Church*. W. B. Eerdmans Publishing Co. 1955. An exegetical study of the major passages of Scripture dealing with the people of God.

Kuiper, R. B. *The Glorious Body of Christ*. Wm. B. Eerdmans Publishing Co. 1958. S systematic study of the Church, her officers, and opportunities.

Richards, L. O. *A New Face for the Church*. Zondervan Publishing House. 1970. A look at the church of the future.

——. *Tomorrow's Church Today*. N.A.E. 1968. A call to faith—and change, in order to meet the present needs of the world. Oriented toward Christian education.

Stewardship

Ammerman. *Golden Ladder of Stewardship*. Baker.

Briggs, E. A., and Cryer, N. S. *Christian Idea of Stewardship*. Abingdon.

Byfield, R. *Your Money and Your Church*. Doubleday. 1959.

Catherwood, H. F. R. *The Christian in Industrial Society*. IV Press.

Fuller, Reginold H. and Rice, B. *Christianity and the Affluent Society*. Wm. B. Eerdmans Publishing Co. 1967.

Howell, R. W. *Saved to Serve: Accent on Stewardship*. Baker. 1967.

Muncey, W. L., Jr. *Trustees of Creation*. Judson Press. 1949.

Rolston, H. *Stewardship in the New Testament Church*. John Knox Press. 1947.

Salstrand, G. A. *Tithe: The Minimal Standard for Christian Giving*. Baker.
Simpson, J. E. *This Grace Also*. Fleming H. Revell. 1933.
Vischer, L. *Tithing in the Early Church*. Fortress. 1966.

The Fruit

Burroughs, J. *The Rare Jewel of Christian Contentment*. Banner of Truth Trust. 1964.
Bittinger, A. *Gifts and Grace*. Wm. B. Eerdmans Publishing Co. 1968.
Beach, W. *Christian Life*. John Knox.
Edwards, J. *Charity and Its Fruits*. Banner of Truth Trust. 1969.
Lewis, C. S. *The Four Loves*. Harcourt, Brace. 1960.
Spring. *The Distinguishing Traits of Christian Character*. Presbyterian and Reformed Publishing Co.

Scripture Index